THE CAMBRIDGE ANCIENT HISTORY

FOURTH VOLUME OF PLATES

THE
CAMBRIDGE
ANCIENT HISTORY

EDITED BY

S. A. COOK, Litt.D., F.B.A.

F. E. ADCOCK, M.A.

M. P. CHARLESWORTH, M.A.

VOLUME OF PLATES IV

PREPARED BY

C. T. SELTMAN, M.A.

CAMBRIDGE

AT THE UNIVERSITY PRESS

1966

PUBLISHED BY
THE SYNDICS OF THE CAMBRIDGE UNIVERSITY PRESS
Bentley House, 200 Euston Road, London, N.W.1
American Branch: 32 East 57th Street, New York, N.Y. 10022

First printed 1934
Reprinted 1960
1966

Printed in Great Britain at the University Printing House, Cambridge
(Brooke Crutchley, University Printer)

PREFACE

The greater part of this volume is occupied with illustrations of Italic art and of the art produced under the Julio-Claudian Emperors. In an earlier volume Etruscan art was illustrated and discussed in connection with the culture of that people in the day of their power; in this will be found instances of the Etruscan work that has its place more particularly in the shaping of art in the Italian peninsula which was to end by becoming Roman.

The three earlier volumes of plates laid a certain emphasis on the formation, growth, and diffusion of the artistic ideas of the Greeks. Now Greek art no longer fills the front of the scene; but even thus Greek models were factors of significance in the formation of Roman sculpture, and influenced at times the Roman art of portraiture. This is patent during the late Republican and Augustan periods when the Roman taste for sculpture was being formed. And, even after the Romans had ceased to be learners, some of the more attractive portraiture, like the Agrippa of Buthrotum, the Emperor Gaius in Copenhagen, and the bronze prince in New York, was Hellenistic in origin and feeling. This, however, occasions no surprise; for Greece was an integral part of the Empire, and Greek artists and craftsmen must have been largely employed in the capital. So far, however, as the negative evidence of literary and epigraphic sources goes, Greeks were, it seems, responsible chiefly for statues and copies made as ornaments for the villas and houses of the Romans or the public squares of the city. The decorative sculpture of Imperial arches, columns, and similar monuments remained anonymous, and here the Greek element, though not wholly absent, is more difficult to trace. In the fields of painting and architecture we know of celebrated Romans, for these were concerned with arts that had a long history in Rome; and in architecture, at any rate, the Greek genius was surpassed by the Roman. The most imposing achievements of the architects of Rome will, however, find a place in the fifth and last of these volumes of plates.

Seven plates devoted to the Parthians show their debt to Greece and to Mesopotamia, while there are aspects of their work which mark it as a fruitful contributor to the art that was to arise in New Rome.

The subjects illustrated have been selected and commented on by the writers of various chapters in volumes ix and x of the *Cambridge Ancient History*. Mr Hignett has dealt with the products of the Celts, Dr Tarn with the art and architecture of the Parthians; and I am responsible for the descriptions of the coins, the choice of which has been made by the writers of various historical chapters. The volume, however, owes by far the greatest debt to Mrs Strong, who has chosen for illustration and comment numerous little-known and some unpublished products of Italic and Roman art, in addition to the more celebrated examples. She has felt it desirable to write a certain number of full commentaries because information about the art of these periods is dispersed among many different publications, some of them difficult of access.

Mrs Strong wishes to thank those scholars who have helped with photographs and in various other ways; Professors Anti, Bartoli, Bocconi, Boethius, Cultrera, Delbrück, Giglioli, Lehmann-Hartleben, Dottoressa A. Levi and Professor Doro Levi, Dr Lugli, Professors Maiuri and Marconi, Dr Matz, Monsieur Michon, Professors Rizzo, Sieveking, Tomassetti, Ugolini, and Weickert.

She also desires to express her regret that Professor Levi's article on the 'Tomba della Pellegrina[1]' in Chiusi and kindred subjects were not known to her in time to make use of them in her descriptions of the plates illustrative of Etrusco-Italic art.

The Editors wish to join with Mrs Strong in expressing especial gratitude to Dr L. Curtius for the generous way in which he has permitted the use of material from the superb photographic collection of the German Institute in Rome. They are also grateful for illustrations and plaster casts contributed by the Directors of the British Museum, the Staatliche Museen in Berlin, the Cabinet de Médailles of the Bibliothèque Nationale, the Museum of Fine Arts in Boston, the Fitzwilliam Museum in Cambridge, the Colchester Museum, the Ny Carlsberg Glyptotek and the National Museum in Copenhagen, the Altertums Museum of Mainz, the

---

[1] *Rivista del R. Istituto di Archeologia e Storia del Arte*, iv, 1932–3, pp. 7 *sqq.*, 101 *sqq.*

PREFACE

Metropolitan Museum of New York, and the Kunsthistorisches Museum of Vienna. Help has also been generously given by the Society of Antiquaries, the Associates in Fine Arts at Yale University, the American Academy and the British School in Rome, the German Archaeological Institute, the Ufficio Antichità e Belle Arti of the Governatorato of Rome, and by Professor A. B. Cook, Monsieur R. Jameson, Mr E. T. Newell, Professors D. M. Robinson, Rostovtzeff, and Sarre. Finally I wish to thank Mr E. S. G. Robinson for permission to incorporate a suggestion of his about the Gortynian coin of Metellus, and Professor Minns and Mr Mattingly for their help with Bosporan and Roman coins.

Reproductions have been allowed by the following publishers:
F. Bruckmann, A.G., Munich (Brunn, *Denkmäler*).
Giesecke and Devrient, Leipzig (Furtwängler, *Die Antiken Gemmen*).
W. de Gruyter and Co., Berlin (*Jahrbuch des deutschen archäol. Instituts*).
K. W. Hiersemann, Leipzig (Pič-Déchelette, *Le Hradischt de Stradonic*).
U. Hoepli, Milan (*Monumenti dei Lincei*).
Libreria del Stato, Rome (Maiuri, *Casa di Menandro*).
E. Leroux, Paris (*Monuments Piot*).
Macmillan and Co., London (*Papers of the British School in Rome*).
Seemann and Co., Leipzig (Curtius, *Die Wandmalerei Pompejis*).
Tournier, Tunis (Poinssot, *L'Autel de la Gens Augusta*).

The Staff of the University Press have been constantly helpful with their accustomed care and skill. The design on the outside cover is after the bronze statuette of a Lar, reproduced by permission of Monsieur Michon of the Department of Greek and Roman Antiquities in the Louvre.*

C.T.S.

October 1934

---

* This sentence refers to a jacket design which has been superseded.

TABLE OF CONTENTS

ix

CONTENTS

CONTENTS

xi

CONTENTS

CONTENTS

CONTENTS

The following works are generally referred to by *the name of the author only*.

BIANCHI BANDINELLI, R. *Testa in terracotta del Museo di Berlino*, in *Mnemosyne*, 1934, pp. 81 *sqq.*

DELLA SETA, A. *Italia Antica*, Bergamo, 1928 (referred to as *I.A.*).

DUCATI, P. *Storia dell' Arte Etrusca*, Florence, 1927.

GOETHERT, F. W. *Zur Kunst der römischen Republik*, Berlin, 1931.

HAUSENSTEIN, W. *Das Bild. Atlanten zur Kunst*, 2. *Die Bildnerei der Etrusker*, Munich, 1922.

HEKLER, A. *Greek and Roman Portraits*, London, 1912.

HELBIG-AMELUNG. *Führer durch die Sammlungen Klassischer Altertümer in Rom*, Leipzig, 1912.

KASCHNITZ-WEINBERG, G. *Studien zur etruskischen und frührömischen Porträtkunst*, in *Römische Mitteilungen*, XLI, 1926, pp. 133 *sqq.*

—— *Bemerkungen zur Struktur der alt-italischen Plastik*, in *Studii Etruschi*, VII, 1933, pp. 135 *sqq.* (referred to as *Bemerkungen*).

KLUGE, K. und K. LEHMANN-HARTLEBEN. *Die antiken Grossbronzen*. 3 vols. Berlin and Leipzig, 1927.

KÖRTE, G. *Rilievi delle urne Etrusche*, Berlin, 1890.

MÜHLESTEIN, A. *Die Kunst der Etrusker*, Berlin, 1929.

NOGARA, B. *Gli Etruschi e la loro Civiltà*, Milan, 1933.

PARIBENI, R. *Il Ritratto nell' Arte Antica*, Milan, 1934.

PLATNER-ASHBY. *A Topographical Dictionary of Ancient Rome*, Oxford, 1929.

RANDALL-MACIVER, D. *The Etruscans*, Oxford, 1927.

RIZZO, G. E. *La Pittura Ellenistico-Romana*, Milan, 1929.

SPINAZZOLA. *Le Arte Decorative in Pompei*, 1928.

SWINDLER, M. H. *Ancient Painting*, New Haven-London, 1929.

VAN ESSEN, C. C. *Chronologie van de Romeinsche Sculptuur tijdens de Republik*, in *Mededeelingen van het Nederlandsch Historisch Instituut te Rome*, VIII, 1928.

WEEGE, F. *Oskische Grabmalerei*, in *J.D.A.I.* XXIV, 1909, 3, pp. 99 *sqq.*

WEST, R. *Römische Porträt-Plastik*, Munich, 1933.

ZADOKS-JOSEPHUS JITTA, A. *Ancestral Portraiture in Rome, and the art of the last century of the Republic*. Allard Pierson Stifting, Amsterdam, 1932.

1

[a] *Eunus*, leader of the Servile War in Sicily, *c.* 135 B.C., self-styled 'King Antiochus.' Bronze coin minted at *Enna*. Veiled head of Demeter to right. Rev. BACIANTIO, ear of corn. *British Museum.* (ix, 13.)

[b], [c] Denarii issued by the Italians in the *Social War*, *c.* 90 B.C. [b] Head of ITALIA Laureate. Rev. Q · [Pompaedius] SILO, eight warriors swearing alliance. [c] 'Multi embratur.' Rev. 'C. Paapi' (*i.e.* C. Papius Mutilus imperator). Head of Bacchus and the Italian bull goring the Roman wolf. [b] *Bibl. Nat. Paris*, Wt. 3·45 g.; [c] *Brit. Mus.* Wt. 3·83 g. (ix, 185, 187.)

[d], [e], [f] Denarii with serrate edges struck *c.* 117 B.C., probably on the occasion of the foundation of *Narbo Martius*. The types are helmeted head of goddess, moneyer's name. Rev. In biga a warrior with Gallic arms and trumpet, beneath L · LIC [inius Crassus]. CN · DOM [itius Ahenobarbus], Commissioners for the foundation. *Brit. Mus.* (ix, 113.) See also 86 below.

[g] Aureus perhaps minted in Spain, *c.* 76 B.C., by *Pompey*, with types referring to his exploits in Africa in 81 B.C. MAGNVS head of Africa in elephant-skin cap, ewer, lituus. Rev. PRO · COS Pompey as triumphator. *Brit. Mus.* Wt. 8·93 g. (ix, 278.)

[h] Bronze coin of *Jannaeus Alexander*, 103–76 B.C. Greek and Hebrew legends: types, Seleucid anchor and wheel. *Brit. Mus.* (ix, 398.)

[i] Bronze coin of *Mattathiah Antigonus*, King and High Priest in Jerusalem, 40 B.C. Hebrew and Greek legends: types, cornucopiae and wreath. *Brit. Mus.* (ix, 405; x, 48.)

[j] Bronze coin struck at *Zacynthus*, *c.* 36 B.C., by *C. Sosius* for Antony. ZA [cynthus], head of Antony. Rev. Trophy between Jewish captives; an allusion to the capture of Jerusalem by Sosius in 37 B.C. *Brit. Mus.* (ix, 406; x, 52, 54.)

[k]–[o] Kings of Pontus. [k] Gold stater of *Mithridates II* with Alexander-types, early third century. [l] Tetradrachm of *Mithridates III*. Portrait. Rev. Zeus, as on the Alexander coinage, *c.* 250 B.C. [m] *Pharnaces I*, *c.* 180 B.C., tetradrachm. Portrait. Rev. Iranian deity. (ix, 224.) [n] *Mithridates IV*, *c.* 170 B.C., tetradrachm. Portrait. Rev. Perseus. [o] *Mithridates IV and Laodice*, tetradrachm. Conjoined portraits. Rev. Zeus and Hera. [k]–[m], [o] *Bibl. Nat. Paris*, Wts. 8·48; 17·15; 17·05; 17·05 g. [n] *Jameson Coll.* Wt. 17·1 g. (ix, 221, 223 *sq.*)

[b]

[a]

[c]

[d]

[e]

[f]

[g]

[h]

[i]

[j]

[k]

[l]

[k]

[m]

[n]

[o]

1-2

[a]–[c] Coinage of *Asia* with the King's portrait. (ix, 224.) [a] Tetradrachm. Rev. Stag grazing, star and crescent, royal name and titles, date and monogram, all in ivy-wreath. *Bibl. Nat. Paris,* Wt. 17 g. [b] Gold stater, as [a] but with two monograms. *Jameson Coll.* Wt. 8·39 g. [c] Tetradrachm as [a] but Pegasus in place of stag. *Jameson Coll.* Wt. 16·3 g.

[d], [e] Coinage in *Athens*, 87 B.C. (ix, 246.) [d] Gold stater. Head of Athena Parthenos. Rev. Owl on Amphora ΑΘΕ · ΒΑΣΙΛΕ ΜΙΘΡΑΔΑΤΗΣ, ΑΡΙΣΤΙΩΝ, star and two crescents, all in olive-wreath. *Brit. Mus.* Wt. 8·23 g. [e] Tetradrachm as last but ΑΡΙΣΤΙΩΝ, ΦΙΛΩΝ, Pegasus in field. *Seltman Coll.* Wt. 16·52 g.

[f]–[i] Gold staters issued in various cities of the Euxine sea-board with types of Lysimachus (see *Volume of Plates* ii, 8 [l]) but with the Alexander-head resembling the head of Mithridates. Rev. Athena Nikephoros, etc. [f] minted in Byzantium, [g] in Calchedon, [h] in Tomi, [i] in Istrus. *Bement, Petrowicz* (2) *Collections*, and *Commerce*, Wts. 8·44; 8·31; 8·20; 8·21 g. (ix, 232.)

[j]–[o] Bronze of various cities of the Pontic Empire. [j]–[l] Head of Ares. Rev. Sword in sheath. [m], [n] Head of Apollo. Rev. Thyrsus and tripod. [o] Head of Dionysus. Rev. Thyrsus and cista. [j] Laodicea; *Bibl. Nat. Paris.* [k] Amastris; *ib.* [m] Panticapaeum; *Seltman Coll.* [n] Gorgippia; *Berlin.* [l], [o] Amisus; *Berlin* and *Milan.* (ix, 222, 232, 237.)

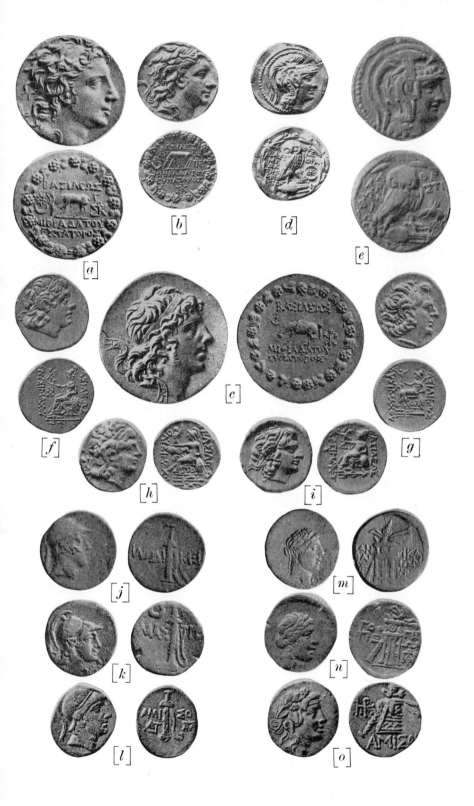

[a]

[b]

[d]

[e]

[c]

[f]

[g]

[h]

[i]

[j]

[m]

[k]

[n]

[l]

[o]

COINS OF RULERS OF PAPHLAGONIA,
BITHYNIA AND CAPPADOCIA

[a]–[c] Paphlagonia. [a] *Pylamenes, c.* 133 B.C., bronze. Head of Heracles. Rev. Nike. [b] *Deiotarus Philadelphus and Adobogiona, c.* 31 to 5 B.C., drachm. Two portraits. [c] *Deiotarus Philadelphus and Deiotarus Philopator,* bronze. Portrait. Rev. Caps of the Dioscuri. [a] *Bibl. Nat. Paris;* [b] *Berlin,* Wt. 3·81 g.; [c] *Brit. Mus.*

[d]–[h] Bithynia. [d] *Nicomedes I, c.* (?) 279–255 B.C., tetradrachm. Portrait. Rev. Female holding spears seated on rock, shield beside her. [e] *Ziaelas, c.* (?) 255–235 B.C., bronze. Portrait. Rev. Trophy. [f] *Prusias I, c.* (?) 238–183 B.C., tetradrachm. Portrait. Rev. Zeus. [g] *Prusias II, c.* 183–149 B.C., tetradrachm; types as last. [h] *Nicomedes II,* 149–120 B.C., gold stater. Portrait. Rev. Armed horseman. [d] *Bibl. Nat. Paris,* Wt. 16·94 g.; [e] *Berlin;* [f] *Bibl. Nat. Paris,* Wt. 16·44 g.; [g] *ib.* Wt. 16·71 g.; [h] *ib.* Wt. 8·38 g.

[i]–[q] Cappadocia. [i] *Ariarathes IV,* 220–163 B.C., drachm; [j] *Ariarathes V,* 163–130 B.C., tetradrachm; [k] *Ariarathes VI, c.* (?) 125–111 B.C., drachm; [l] *Ariarathes VII, c.* (?) 111–99 B.C., drachm. All with portraits, and reverse Athena Nikephoros. [m], [n] *Ariarathes VIII Eusebes Philopator,* a son of Mithridates VI of Pontus (called Ariarathes IX by Head, *Hist. Num.*[2] p. 751), 99–87 B.C. His tetradrachm [n] repeats the reverse type of his father's coinage; see 4 [c] above. The drachm [m] repeats the reverse of the normal Cappadocian regal coinage. Both have a youthful portrait. (ix, 236.) [o] *Ariobarzanes I Philoromaios,* 95–62 B.C., drachm; [p] *Ariobarzanes II,* 62–52 B.C., drachm; [q] *Ariobarzanes III,* 52–42 B.C., drachm. Usual types. All in *Brit. Mus.* Wts. 4·11; 15·97; 3·95; 3·99; 3·98; 16·72; 4·14; 4·43; 2·96 g. (ix, 235.)

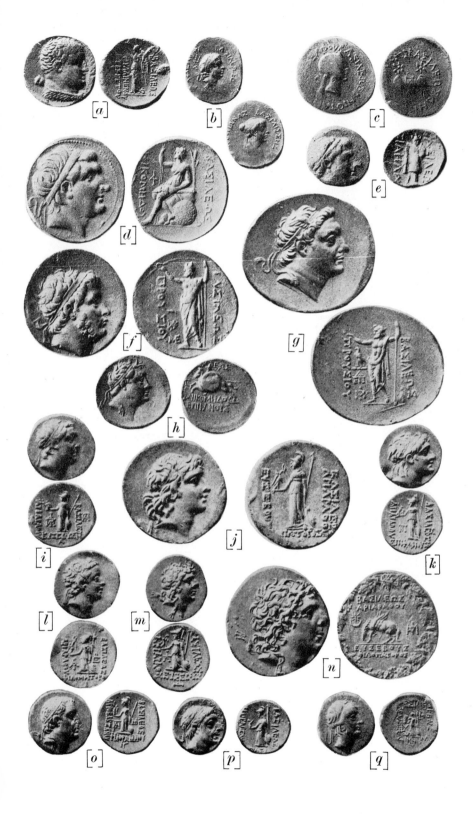

[a] *Tiridates I, c.* 248 to after 227 B.C., drachm. Head of a king in pointed Saca cap. Rev. Deified beardless archer seated on omphalos. Compare Seleucid Apollos, *Volume of Plates* iii, 12 [f], [g]. (ix, 589, 591, 594.) [b] *Mithridates II*, 124–87 B.C., drachm. King bearded and wearing Greek diadem. Rev. Archer as before but on throne. (ix, 591.)

[c], [d] Feign of Mithridates II drachms, with types as last, struck for an eastern campaign and inscribed **ΚΑΤΑCΤΡΑΤΕΙΑ** and **ΤΡΑΞΙΑΝΗ**. (ix, 585.)

[e], [f] *Mithridates I*, before 160–138 B.C., coins of Hellenizing style. [e] Tetradrachm. Diademed portrait. Rev. Heracles. [f] Bronze. Rev. Elephant, a Seleucid type. Compare *Volume of Plates* ii, 10 [b]. (ix, 591.) All in *Brit. Mus.* Wts. 3·97; 3·82; 3·45; 3·33; 15·62 g.

[g] *Himerus*, 124/3 B.C., tetradrachm perhaps minted in Babylon. Portrait. Rev. **ΒΑCΙΛΕΩC ΜΕΓΑΛΟΥ ΑΡCΑΚΟΥ ΝΙΚΗΦΟΡΟΥ**, Dionysus Nikephoros, calathus on head, cornucopiae in left hand, enthroned. (ix, 584.) *Newell Coll.* Wt. 16·22 g. [h]–[k] Bronze coins minted by *Hyspaosines* King of *Characene*, who ruled in Babylon in 127 and 126 B.C. The original types were diademed beardless head. Rev. Anchor of Seleucid type. (Note head on [h]; **ΥΕΠΛΟ** on [j], [k].) All known specimens are overstruck by *Mithridates II* in 122/1 B.C. with types; bearded head. Rev. Cornucopiae. *Newell Coll.* (ix, 584.) [l] *Orodes II*, 57–56 B.C., drachm. Types as [b]–[d] countermarked by an Indian-Parthian king. (ix, 599.)

[m], [n] Persis. [m] *Autophradates I*, second century B.C., tetradrachm. Head in *kyrbasia* tied with diadem. Rev. Great Zoroastrian fire-altar, king on right, banner of Kava on left, Ahuramazda above. [n] *Darius II*, first century B.C., drachm. Head in Parthian cap (cf. 10 [e] below). Rev. King beside small Parthian altar. *Brit. Mus.* Wts. 16·39; 4·0 g. (ix, 586, 594 *sq.*)

[o] *Labienus.* Denarius, *c.* 40 B.C. Q · LABIENVS · PARTHICVS · IMP · his portrait. Rev. Light Parthian horse with quiver slung from the saddle. *Brit. Mus.* Wt. 3·78 g. (ix, 601; x, 47.)

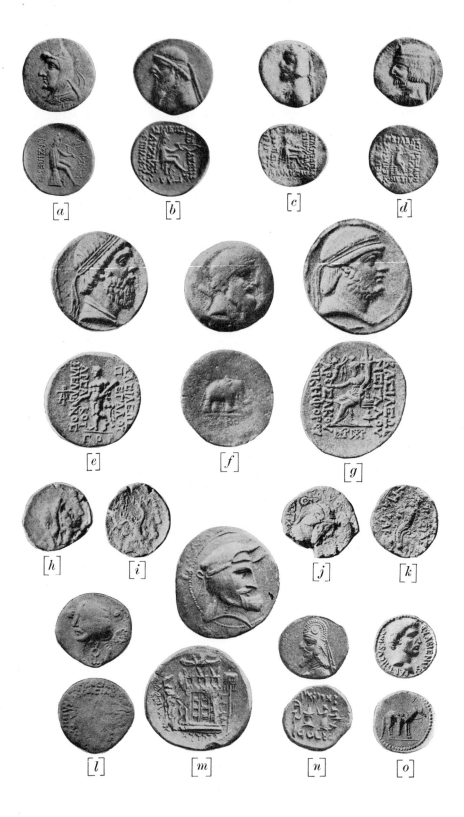

[a] [b] [c] [d]

[e] [f] [g]

[h] [i] [j] [k]

[l] [m] [n] [o]

COINS OF PARTHIA, INDIA, GAUL,
AND CENTRAL GREECE

[a] Parthia. *Artabanus II, c.* 129–124 B.C., tetradrachm of Greek idealistic style. Diademed bust. Rev.: Tyche Nikephoros. *Brit. Mus.* Wt. 15·16 g. [b] Characene. *Tiraeus I*, tetradrachm of 90–89 B.C. Realistic portrait of aged king. Rev. as last. *Bibl. Nat. Paris,* Wt. 15 g. (ix, 591, 600.)

[c], [d] *Mithridates III*, 56–55 B.C., for a brief spell drove out his elder brother Orodes II and struck tetradrachms with his own name, the first Arsacid to do so. *Orodes II*, reinstated in 55 B.C.,] overstruck his brother's coins. On [c], an overstruck specimen, **ΜΙΘΡΑΔΑΤΟΥ** is visible between **ΕΠΙΦΑΝΟΥΣ** and **ΦΙΛΕΛ-ΛΗΝΟΣ**. [d] is an ordinary tetradrachm of Orodes II. Rev. The Tyche of Seleuceia kneeling to the king. *Berlin*, Wts. 15·16; 15·0 g. (ix, 604.) [e], [f] Examples of Parthian headdress; drachms of *Pacorus II*, A.D. 92/93, and *Vardanes II*, A.D. 55. *Brit. Mus.* Wts. 3·77; 3·80 g. (ix, 589.)

[g]–[j] Coins of the Kushans in Northern India. *Kanishka, King of Kings*, first to second century A.D. On the obverse of all four is a figure of the king, a small altar beside him; his costume is like that of the Parthians (see 22 [a], 26 [a] below). On the reverses are various deities: [g] gold stater, *Athro*, a Persian fire-god; [h] bronze, *Helios*; [i] gold stater, *Shiv*, four-armed; [j] gold stater, *Buddha*. All in *Brit. Mus.* Wts. 7·96; —; 7·97; 7·08 g. (ix, 595.)

[k]–[m] Gaul. [k] Pale electrum, Roman denarius standard; types, degraded head and biga derived from those of Philip II of Macedon. Assigned to the *Aulerci Eburovices*. [l] Silver of the *Caletes* ATEVL. Head copied from a denarius. Rev. VLATOS, animal seated. [m] Silver ΓΙΧΤΙL as last. Rev. Monster attacking man. *Naville Catal.* v, Wts. 3·44; 1·75; 3·29 g. (ix, 539.)

[n]–[p] *Sulla* in Greece after the battles of Chaeronea and Orchomenus, 86 B.C. [n] Tetradrachm with Athenian types but uninscribed; the owl between two trophies. [o] Aureus, [p] denarius. L SVLLA, head of Venus, Cupid with palm-branch. Rev. IMPER ITERVM. Lituus and simpulum between two trophies. *Brit. Mus.* Wts. 17·06; 10·73; 3·66 g.

10

[a] [b] [c] [d] [e] [f] [g] [h] [i] [j] [k] [l] [m] [n] [o] [p]

[a] *Gortyn*, 69–64 B.C., in alliance with Q. Caecilius Metellus, tetradrachm. **POMAΣ**, head of Roma, or idealized portrait of Metellus, an elephant's head (the device of the Caecilli) on the helmet. Rev. **ΓOPTYN**, cult-statue of Ephesian Artemis, bee, elephant's head; all in wreath. *Berlin*, Wt. 11·99 g. (ix, 375.)

[b] *M. Aemilius Scaurus*, Curule Aedile in 58 B.C., with P. Plautius Hypsaeus, denarius. The obverse refers to an episode of 62 B.C. when Scaurus was sent against Aretas King of the Nabataeans. Though the latter obtained good terms Scaurus did not scruple to show the Arab king as a suppliant kneeling beside his camel. Below REX ARETAS. *Brit. Mus.* Wt. 3·76 g. (ix, 383.)

[c] *Pompeiopolis*, formerly Soli, in Cilicia, refounded in 66 B.C., bronze. Head of Pompey. Rev. Athena Nikephoros of Soli. *Brit. Mus.* (ix, 394.)

[d]–[h] *Julius Caesar*. [d] Aureus of 46 B.C.C · CAESAR COS · TER, a veiled head. Rev. A · HIRTIVS · PR, lituus, ewer and axe. *Brit. Mus.* Wt. 7·91 g. (ix, 689.) [e] Denarius issued in 44 B.C. by the moneyer P · SEPVLLIVS MACER. Obv. CLEMENTIAE CAESARIS, a picture of the temple to his clemency which was to have been built. *Brit. Mus.* Wt. 3·86 g. (ix, 719.) [f] Denarius of the moneyers Cossutius and Maridianus, 44 B.C. Obv. CAESAR PARENS PATRIAE, his head veiled and laureate. (ix, 720, 722, 727.) [g] Denarius, 44 B.C. Head as last. CAESAR DICT · PERPETVO. Rev. Moneyer as on [e], figure of Venus Victrix. (ix, 722, 727.) [h] Denarius, 44 B.C., legend as last, head laureate. Rev. L · BVCA, caduceus, fasces, exa, globe, and clasped hands. (ix, 722, 727, 734.) The three last, formerly *Bement Coll.*

[i] *Tigranes of Armenia* ruling in Antioch, 83–69 B.C., tetradrachm. Portrait of king in lofty tiara decorated with sun between two eagles (compare p. 20 [a] below). Rev. Tyche of Antioch, river Orontes swimming at her feet (compare *Volume of Plates* iii, 124). *Brit. Mus.* Wt. 16·45 g. (ix, 357.)

[j] *Brutus*. Denarius, 42 B.C., minted in Macedon. Head of Brutus. Rev. EID · MAR, cap of Liberty between two daggers. *Brit. Mus.* Wt. 3·8 g. (ix, 727; x, 19.)

[k], [l] Portraits of *Cleopatra* on tetradrachms minted outside Egypt. On the reverse of the former a Ptolemaic eagle; on the latter a portrait of Antony. [k] Ascalon, 30 B.C. [l] Antioch (?). *Brit. Mus.* Wts. 13·04; 14·32 g.

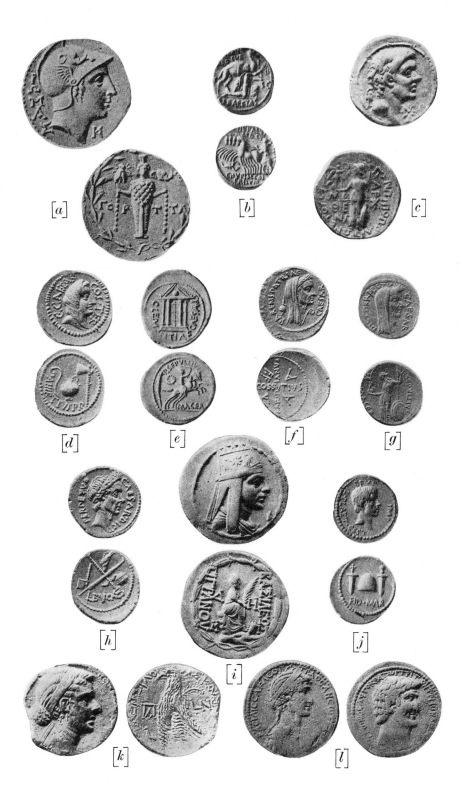

[a]　　　　　　[b]　　　　　[c]

[d]　　　　[e]　　　　[f]　　　　[g]

[h]　　　　　[i]　　　　　[j]

[k]　　　　　[l]

[*a*] PEDESTAL URN with raised ribs; late Celtic, beginning of the first century B.C., from a grave found at *Shoebury*, Essex, in 1904. Now in the *Colchester Museum*. Others have been found at Aylesford and Swarling in Kent, and elsewhere. Compare J. Déchelette, *Manuel*, II, 3, p. 1487, fig. 1; C. Hawkes and G. C. Dunning in *Archaeol. Journal*, 87 (1930), pp. 150 *sqq.* (ix, 538.)
[*Photograph Colchester Museum*]

[*b*] A SWORD, SCABBARD, and BROOCHES of the Late La Tène period. For the two former see J. Déchelette, *Manuel*, II, 3, p. 1114; for the brooches, from *Swarling*, see J. P. Bushe-Fox, *Excavations of the Late-Celtic Urn-Field at Swarling, Kent,* in *Reports of the Research Committee of the Society of Antiquaries,* No. 5 (1925).

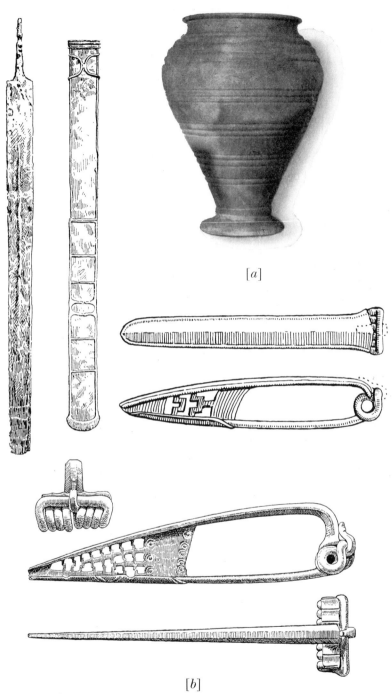

[a]

[b]

POTTERY. In the second half of the first century B.C. the painted vases found in Central Gaul correspond in general type of decoration, if not in every detail, with this pottery found at *Stradonitz* in Bohemia, and now in the Museum at *Prague*. The bands are usually red in colour, the chequers and wavy lines in grey-black, on a whitish ground. (ix, 539.)

[J. L. Pič and J. Déchelette, *Le Hradischt de Stradonic en Bohème et les fouilles de Bibracte*, 1901, Pl. XLIX]

[*a*] The upper halves of two VICTORIES from *Doura*, in the *Louvre*. They are made of plaster, and hold palm-branches, the one in her left, the other in her right hand.
[*Photograph Giraudon*]

[*b*] A VICTORY painted in tempera in brilliant colours on one of a pair of folding wooden doors which enclosed a shrine of the Tyche of Doura; found at *Doura*. She wears the same type of dress and coiffure as the two plaster Victories, and carries wreath and palm-branch. In one aspect this art may be described as decadent Hellenistic; but from another point of view the tall slender figure, with its frontal head and brilliant formal colouring, appears as a forerunner of the greater art of the Byzantines. Second to third century A.D. (ix, 589, 600.)
[From a reconstruction in *The Bulletin of the Association in Fine Arts at Yale University*, February 1930]

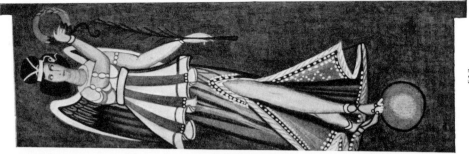

[b]

[a]

2-2

[*a*] HATRA. Part of a carved frieze representing the radiate facing head of the Sun-god between two eagles. Compare the sun between eagles on the tiara worn by Tigranes of Armenia upon coins minted in Antioch (12 [*i*]). First century A.D.

[*b*] HATRA. A wall in the south hall of the principal palace; the shallow buttresses ornamented with masks of Graeco-Parthian style. First century A.D. (ix, 592, 600.)
[*Photographs Professor Sarre*]

[a]

[b]

[*a*] Cast from a CLAY MOULD, width 12·5 centimetres, in the Kaiser Friedrich Museum, *Berlin*. A Parthian noble, with frizzed hair, a long coat of mail, trousers, and a sword, stands beside a pillared and arched shrine within which is standing Tyche of Hellenistic type. She wears a tall headdress and raises her right hand.

[*Photograph Professor Sarre*]

[*b*] Parthian bronze STATUETTE of a nude goddess (Anaitis?) height 11·5 centimetres, in *Berlin*. The coiffure is elaborate. (ix, 589.)

[*Photograph Berlin Museums*]

[a]

[b]

Graeco-Assyrian PORTRAIT head of MITHRIDATES I, in greenish-black serpentine. Height 0·09 m. *c.* 160–138 B.C. In the D. M. Robinson Collection, in *Baltimore*. He wears a diadem of Greek type tied at the back and with the ends hanging down. The eyes were set in separately. See *American Journal of Archaeology*, 1927, pp. 338 *sqq.*; and compare the coins of Mithridates, 8 [*e*], [*f*] above. (ix, 600.)

[*Photographs Professor D. M. Robinson*]

THE PARTHIANS

THREE GRAFFITI FROM DOURA

[*a*] A Parthian foot-soldier with a heavy spear, long sword, typical helmet, leather armour, and baggy trousers. He is perhaps intended to be standing on the decapitated head of an enemy.

[*b*] A Parthian horseman shooting an arrow. His head is frontal and the hair resembles that of the noble, 22 [*a*].

[*c*] A Parthian knight in full armour on a heavy charger which is covered in chain mail. The rider has a tall metal helmet with vizor, wears a coat of chain-mail, and apparently metal greaves; he carries a sword and a long spear. There are no stirrups. (ix, 601.)

[*Drawings reproduced by permission of the Associates in Fine Arts at Yale University*]

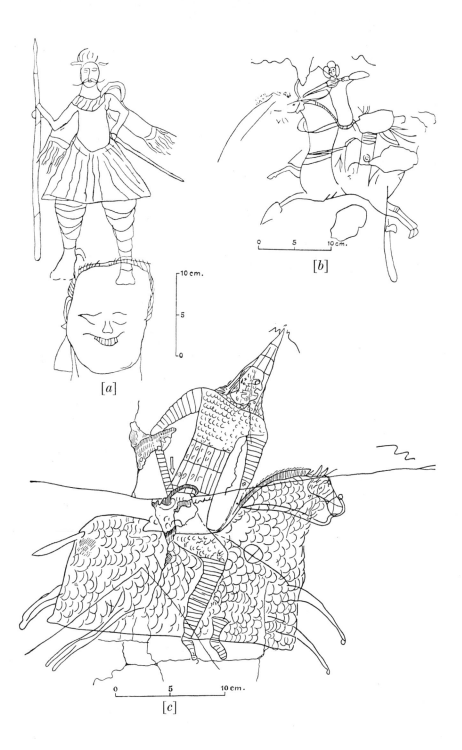

[a]

[b]

[c]

[a] DOURA. General view of a part of the walls and the citadel.

[b] DOURA. A street inside the city leading to the Palmyrene Gate. (ix, 595 *sq.*, 599 *sq.*)
[*Photographs Madame Rostovtzeff*]

[a]

[b]

[a], [b] Parthian influence was considerable in Northern Syria. King Antiochus I of Commagene, 69–34 B.C., set up CARVED RELIEFS at *Nimrud Dag* representing some of his ancestors, and himself as a worshipper of Mithras. The ancestor and the god wear caps resembling the earlier Parthian head-wear (cf. 8 [a]), Antiochus has a tiara like that of the Armenian Tigranes (12 [i]). (ix, 224, 589.)
[*Photographs Professor Sarre*]

[c] Bronze coin of *Ariaramnes* of *Cappadocia*, c. 280–230 B.C. The king's head to right in a headdress of Persian type. Rev. **APIAPAMNOY**, horseman.

[d] Bronze coin of a Dynast, Dsari..., of *Anisa* in Cappadocia. Third century B.C. Head as on last. Rev. **ΑΝΙΣΑ, ΔΣΑΡΙ**. The upper part of a goddess facing between two sphinxes, each crowned with a *polos*. Both coins in *Berlin*.

[a]

[b]

[c]

[d]

[*a*], [*b*] Heads of the APOLLO and of the HERMES; from the 'Contest for the Sacred Hind.' The Apollo alone (with detail of head) is illustrated in *Vol. of Plates*, i, 334; but the two heads are reproduced here to show their curiously individual expression: mouth, eyes, chin, facial oval, etc. differing in both. For a new characterization of the statue see Kaschnitz-Weinberg, *Bemerkungen*, pp. 168 *sqq.* From the Capitolium, *Veii.*

[*Photographs: Anderson* [*a*]*; Alinari* [*b*]]

[*c*], [*d*] Two GORGON ANTEFIXES from the same temple. Note the subtle variations of detail; the fierce *rictus* of [*c*], the heavier lines round the mouth, the tongue more vigorously put out, the snake-locks, etc.

[For the fullest publication of these terracottas, see G. Q. Giglioli, *Denkmäler des Arch. Instituts*, III, 1927. *Photographs L.U.C.E.*]

All in *Rome, Museo di Villa Giulia.* (ix, 807.)

[a]

[b]

[c]

[d]

3-2

[*a*] Two HEADS in TERRACOTTA; from the lids of cinerary caskets. The female head and casket belong together (casket not shown in illustration); the male head seems to have been violently wrenched from its casket, which has not been found. They are of a type already known from those of the Tomba Campana at Veii, and are therefore presumably from the Veientan territory. *Rome, Vatican (Museo Gregoriano).* (ix, 808.)

[Discovered in the 'magazzini' of the Vatican by C. Albizzati, and first published by him, *Diss. P.A.R.A.* 1916, pp. 14 *sqq.*, pl. IV; B. Nogara, p. 243, figs. 132, 133; P. Ducati, p. 190. pl. 67, fig. 202 (woman only)]

[*b*] CANOPIC URN. This is one of the finest urns of its kind. For a description of the head and of its affinities to Roman art see ix, 809. The body of the urn is interesting for the treatment of the handles out of which project rudimentary hands, as though there were a struggle for existence between the mechanical and the human shape. *Arezzo, Museo Civico.*

[*c*] CANOPIC URN seated on chair. Height 0·85 m. Bronze chair richly patterned with three irregular rows of phantastic beasts: (1) winged pegasi with lions' tails, (2) winged lions, (3) winged pegasi and lions intermixed. Border of interlacing palmettes on the base. The actual urn is formed of two half-globes soldered together. The head is of terracotta. First half of sixth century B.C. (?) It is not absolutely certain that the head belongs to the urn. For a characterization see Kaschnitz-Weinberg, *Bemerkungen*, pp. 277 *sqq.* Found at *Dolciano*, near Chiusi. In *Chiusi, Museo Civico.* (ix, 809.)

[H. Mühlestein, p. 214, pl. 125 (with bibl.); D. Randall-MacIver, pp. 227, 236, 241, pl. 43; R. Bianchi Bandinelli, *Dedalo*, vi, 1925, p. 7, and *Mon. Linc.* xxx, 1925, fig. 48; P. Ducati, p. 195, pl. 70, fig. 210; B. Nogara, p. 236, pl. 130. *Photographs Alinari*]

[a]

[b]

[c]

[a] STANDING FEMALE FIGURE (lid of sepulchral urn). The figure, clad in a curious close-fitting garment apparently covered with a net, and a long cloak falling from the shoulders, is interpreted (by Nogara) as leading the groups of mourners which, represented on a much smaller scale, surround the urn (not shown in illustration). *Chiusi, Museo Civico.* (ix, 809.)

[B. Nogara, p. 136, fig. 128; cf. A. Della Seta, p. 240, fig. 250. *Photograph Alinari*]

[b] FEMALE HALF-FIGURE of sandstone (sepulchral urn). Height 0·52 m. Probably a goddess of Death, sometimes interpreted as a goddess of Love. *Chiusi, Museo Civico.* (ix, 809.)

[R. Bianchi Bandinelli, *Dedalo*, vi, pp. 5 *sqq.*; H. Mühlestein, p. 238, fig. 230 (with bibl.); A. Della Seta, *Italia Antica*, p. 242, fig. 256; B. Nogara, p. 325, fig. 189. *Photograph Alinari*]

[c] STANDING MAN (sepulchral urn). Height 1·36 m. The body is hollowed out to receive the ashes. The head serves as a stopper. A himation is wrapped round the body and flung over the left shoulder. The hair, parted in the middle, is bound at the back of the head with a fillet and falls straight to the neck. The short pointed beard, and the hair, pupils and eyelashes are painted black, the flesh red. From *Chianciano*, near Chiusi. *British Museum.* (ix, 809.)

[*B.M. Cat. of Sculpture*, 2nd ed. i, 1, 1931, p. 162, fig. 7]

[d] SEATED MAN (lid of sepulchral urn). Height (with lower half and plinth) 1·38 m. The upper half of the body, against the chair-back, is solid. The lower half (not shown in illustration) is hollowed out to receive the ashes. Forearms missing. Hair combed back behind the ears in regular flutings. Short beard. Traces of paint. Long chiton. From *Chiusi*. *British Museum.* (ix, 809.)

[*B.M. Cat. of Sculpture*, 2nd ed. i, 1, 1931, p. 163, fig. 8 (with bibl.)]

[a]

[c]

[b]

[d]

[*a*] 'OBESUS ETRUSCUS.' Rather more than life-sized. Third century B.C. Lid of alabaster sarcophagus with half-draped recumbent figure wearing the usual funerary wreath and leaning the left elbow on two cushions. In the right hand a patera decorated with a rayed sun. On the left hand a signet ring. *Florence, Museo Archeologico.* (ix, 810.)

[R. West, p. 18, pl. IV, 9; C. Anti, *Studi Etruschi*, IV, p. 167. *Photograph Alinari*]

[*b*] 'LARTH SENTINATES' CAESA.' Third century B.C. Sarcophagus lid of grey-veined white alabaster, with half-draped recumbent figure of a man. Heavy wreaths round neck and head; left hand toys with a large *bulla*; right hand missing. The name *Larth Sentinates' Caesa* is cut on the lid. Found on the right of the entrance of the central *cella* of the Tomba della Pellegrina, *Chiusi*, in 1928. *Chiusi, Tomba della Pellegrina.* (ix, 810.)

[Doro Levi, *Notizie degli Scavi*, 1931, p. 481, fig. XI. *Photograph lent by Professor Doro Levi*]

[*c*] Terracotta lid of ash-chest with PORTRAIT FIGURES. The figures are of an elderly man and his wife engaged in lively argument; the man appearing to listen with something of a puzzled look to the remonstrances of the lady. The group, which has been repeatedly described, passes for a masterpiece of Etruscan portrait-sculpture. *Volterra, Museo Guarnacci.* (ix, 811.)

[A. Hekler, p. 25; A. Della Seta, p. 267, fig. 293; P. Ducati, p. 548, pl. 270, fig. 656; W. Hausenstein, fig. 65; B. Nogara, p. 336 and fig. 210; L. Curtius, *Die Antike*, v, p. 198; G. Karo, *Etruskisch-Römische Bildkunst*, in Antike Plastik, 1928 Festschrift Amelung. *Photograph Alinari*]

[b]

[a]

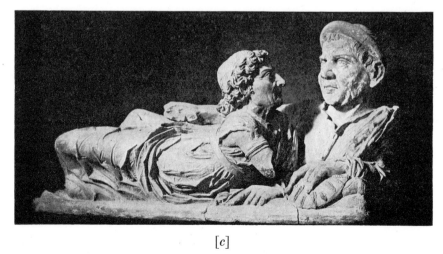

[c]

[*a*] BRONZE HEAD of boy. The face is almost square, with harshly defined planes adjusted without much sense of plasticity. The long striated hair combed to the front is characteristic of a whole group of Italo-Etruscan portrait-heads. *Florence, Museo Archeologico.* (ix, 811.)

[G. Kaschnitz-Weinberg, p. 137, pls. 1, 2; also *Bemerkungen*, p. 184; R. West, p. 18 *sq.*, pl. IV, 8]

[*b*] TERRACOTTA HEAD of young woman. Height 34 cm. End of Republic or early Augustan. The bust is cut below the shoulder as if intended for a niche. The woman wears a soft undergarment cut into a V-shape at the neck, and gathered into a sort of *ruche*; over this is a cloak. Ears pierced for rings. *Rome, Vatican* (*Museo Gregoriano*. (ix, 812.)

[G. Kaschnitz-Weinberg, *Rendiconti P.A.R.A.* III, 1925, p. 346, pl. XXIV; R. Bianchi Bandinelli, p. 87 and fig. 9. *Photographs German Institute*]

[*c*] TERRACOTTA HEAD of young man. Life-size. Reddish-brown terracotta with abundant traces of colour. Long narrow face, broad forehead and somewhat sunken cheeks; hair naturalistically indicated on the surface by the modeller's stick. *Munich.* (ix,812.)

[J. Sieveking, *Münchner Jahrb. der bild. Kunst,* v, 1928, 3, p. 21; R. West, p. 26, pl. VI, 19 and 19*a*; R. Bianchi Bandinelli, p. 95]

[*d*] TERRACOTTA HEAD of young man. Height 30·5 cm.; height of face 16 cm. Similar in character to preceding; eyes long and dreamy; as in the Munich head, the furrows on each side of the nose are deeply marked; like the eyes the mouth is long, and the lips are full. *London, British Museum*; acquired with the Campanari collection? (ix, 812.)

[Unpublished. *Photograph British Museum*]

[a]

[b]

[c]

[d]

[*a*] HEAD OF YOUNG MAN from sarcophagus lid. For long striated locks in Italo-Etruscan manner cf. Florence head and 'Brutus' (42 [*a*], 46). Loosely parted hair over forehead in a fork as in portraits of Augustus. Eyes, nose and closed mouth treated in simple naturalistic manner of the time. *Chiusi, Museo Civico.* (ix, 810.)

[A. Della Seta, p. 267, fig. 292; B. Nogara, p. 336, fig. 216; R. West, p. 19, pl. V, 11]

[*b*] Head of AUGUSTUS. Life-size. The head is shown here for its affinites to Etruscan types. It was made to be let into a statue; the veil, which is drawn over the back of the head, is cut off as in the statue from the Via Labicana. *Chiusi, Museo Civico.* (ix, 810; x, 557.)

[*c*], [*d*] Head of MITHRIDATES. Long known in the Louvre catalogue as 'Roi Grec en Hercule,' but, as F. Winter saw as long ago as 1894, the evidence of coins makes it certain that this is Mithridates VI, Eupator, at the age of about forty. The head is shown here to contrast the πάθος of late Hellenistic art with the simple naturalism of contemporary Italic portraiture. It is a magnificent example of its kind, and in spite of some working over, has all the qualities of an original; its character is essentially Greek. The lion-skin is drawn over the back of the head, the jaw and fangs forming a splendid setting to the brow. It is impossible to identify it among the numbers of portraits of the king which were brought to Rome and Italy as spoils of war (for the silver and gold effigies of Mithridates carried by Pompey in his triumph, see Cic. *Verr.* II, 65, 159, and Pliny, *Nat. Hist.* XXXIII, 12, 151: *triumpho Magni Pompei reperimus translatam . . . argentam statuam . . . Mithridatis Eupatoris*). *Paris, Louvre.* (ix, 815.)

[F. Winter, *J.D.A.I.* IX, 1894, pp. 244 *sqq.*, pl. 8; cf. also E. Pfuhl, *J.D.A.I.* LV, 1930, p. 15, for the school. *Photographs, a, b, Alinari; c, d, Giraudon*]

[a]

[b]

[c]

[d]

BRONZE HEAD, so-called 'Brutus.' Portrait of middle-aged man. The structure is still that of the portrait-heads of the Italic group, such as the Florence boy (42 [a]), though it surpasses them in the magnificent sweep of the line of the skull, and in the severely offset planes of the face. In this head sculpture has progressed beyond the Italic phase and is already Roman. The long pointed locks of hair, the stiff tufts of eyebrows and beard, and the tightly compressed mouth are Italic, but they are rendered with a new precision. The intensity of the gaze likewise is a new note, the head depending largely for its effect on the piercing eyes, which are enamel (white ball, brown iris, encircled in a strip of metal). As already stated in the text, the vividness of the expression may be due to the influence of an ancestral *imago*, made as life-like as possible, either with the help of a death mask or worked up as an imaginary portrait—such an *imago*, if that of a great man, then made permanent in bronze or stone, and set up in some public place, as a full length or as an equestrian statue. Date uncertain, but earlier than Augustus, to whose period the head was formerly assigned. *Rome, Palazzo dei Conservatori.* (ix, 812; x, 557.)

[*B.S.R. Cat. of the Palazzo dei Conservatori*, p. 43, no. 1 (with bibl.) and pl. 60; G. Kaschnitz-Weinberg, p. 138 *sq.*, pls. III–V; R. West, pp. 7 *sq.*, pls. II, 3, 3 *a*, IV, 10; L. Curtius, *Die Antike*, v, 1928, p. 206, fig. 21. *Photograph German Institute*]

[*a*] BRONZE HEAD of young man. Probably broken off a statue; the close leather cap strapped under the chin might equally befit an athlete or priest. The drawing of the cranium, the offset planes apparent under the fleshiness of the face, the harshness of the parts about the temples and the realism of the wisps of hair escaping from the *tutulus*, the lips which, though full, are firmly closed, recall the group of Italo-Etruscan heads. The nose is aquiline; the lips inset. The eyes, now hollow, were, like those of the 'Brutus,' enamel. *British Museum*. (ix, 812.)

[H. B. Walters, *Select Bronzes*, pl. LXVI; cf. *B.M. Cat. of Bronzes*, N. 1614; G. Kaschnitz-Weinberg, p. 145, fig. 6; R. West, p. 23, pl. VII, 16; K. A. Esdaile, *J.R.S.* I, 219, fig. 31 (in this article the Etruscan character of the head was first recognized). *Photograph British Museum*]

[*b*] BRONZE MALE HEAD. A masterpiece of pre-Roman Italic art; the square structure of the face, the line of the cranium, broken only by the wave of the short striated hair; the firmly closed lips and the intensity of the gaze are known from the Etrusco-Italic group, but a fresh realism brings the head very near the 'Brutus.' Inset enamel eyes. Found at *Bovianum Vetus* in Samnium. Paris, *Bibliothèque Nationale*. (ix, 813.)

[G. Kaschnitz-Weinberg, p. 168, fig. 10; R. West, p. 20, pl. V, 13. *Photograph Giraudon*]

[*c*] BRONZE HEAD of a man. The wisp-like hair, the broad planes, the firmly closed lips bring this head into the group of the Florence boy, the 'Brutus' and the head from Bovianum. The iris, which was inset, is missing; eyebrows plastically rendered; face full; heavy chin; deep vertical furrows above the nose. Found in the neighbourhood of *Fiesole*. *Paris, Louvre*. (ix, 812.)

[K. Lehmann-Hartleben, *Antike Grossbronzen*, II, p. 26, fig. 5; G. Kaschnitz-Weinberg, p. 142, fig. XXI, *b*, XXII, *b*,; R. West, p. 21, pl. V, 14. *Photograph Giraudon*]

[*d*] HEAD of 'AULES METILIS.' The derivation of the head from the Italo-Etruscan group is evident, but the Romanization has been carried several stages further. The name of the personage is given in the long inscription (C.I. Etr. 4196) on the edges of the drapery. Found on *Lake Trasimene*. *Florence, Museo Archeologico*. (ix, 813.)

[G. Kaschnitz-Weinberg, p. 182, figs. XXVI, XXVII; L. Milani, *Museo Archeol. di Firenze*, I, p. 136; R. West, p. 38, pls. VIII, 24, and IX, 25; P. Ducati, p. 546, pl. 267, fig. 651. *Photograph German Institute*]

[a]

[b]

[c]

[d]

[*a*] STELE of C. SEPTUMIUS. This excellent work (nose restored) is one of the best examples of a portrait where all the characteristics of a death mask are scrupulously observed, with the exception of the eyes, which in portraits after death-masks were worked up into a semblance of life. The deep furrows round the mouth and nose, the lifeless lips, the salient cheek-bones and denuded cranium are reproduced with great force. The dating has given rise to the most varied opinions. Here the old view of Altmann that the head is late Republican or perhaps even early Augustan is adhered to—a date likewise accepted by Goethert. On the other hand Messerschmidt and Zadoks-Jitta date it to about 80–70 B.C., not taking sufficient account, in the present writer's opinion, of the shape and ample proportions of the toga. For the realistic treatment of the vocal chords, cf. the death-mask head in the Louvre (Zadoks-Jitta, pl. VII, A). Inscr. C. SEPTUMIUS C. F. SAB. IIII. VIR. I. D. Found at *Vulci. Copenhagen, Ny Carlsberg Glyptotek.* (ix, 814.)

[A. Zadoks-Jitta, p. 55, P, pl. XV*a* (for date, p. 73); F. Messerschmidt and A. von Gerkan, *Nekropole von Vulci*, p. 39, fig. 13; F. Poulsen, *Mellem Glyptotekets Romerske Portraetter (Kunstmuseets Aarskrift*, XIII–XVI, 1929), p. 20, fig. 23; *Ny Carlsberg Glyptotek Catalogue*, 556; R. West, p. 50, pl. X, 34; F. W. Goethert, p. 46. *Photograph Ny Carlsberg Glyptotek*]

[*b*] HEAD AFTER A DEATH-MASK. The head (nose entirely restored) was first recognized and published by G. Kaschnitz-Weinberg as being after a death-mask. Recent doubts of its authenticity appear to the present writer, after examination of the head, to be unfounded. It seems to be a genuine example of a death-mask portrait (the eyes worked up as usual), used for a portrait statue or bust (cf. the celebrated 'calvo sacrificante' in the Braccio Nuovo of the Vatican). *Turin, Accademia.* (ix, 814.)

[G. Kaschnitz-Weinberg, p. 191, figs. 23, 24; F. Poulsen, *op. cit.* p. 19. figs. 18, 19, *Photograph German Institute*]

[*c*] DEATH-MASK PORTRAIT. Height 0·23 m. Limestone. Tip of nose, breakages in left eyeball and cheek restored in plaster. An admirable example of death-mask portraiture, showing all the death signs—prominent cheek-bones, drawn and sunken cheeks—with the same fidelity as in the Vulci Septumius (50 [*a*]). *Aquileia.* (ix, 814.)

[F. Poulsen, *Porträtstudien in Nord-Italienischen Provinzmuseen*, p. 12, no. 8, pls. XII–XIII; R. West, p. 51, pl. XI, 39; A. Zadoks-Jitta, p. 54, M, pl. XIII*b*. Photograph *Ny Carlsberg Glyptotek*]

[a]

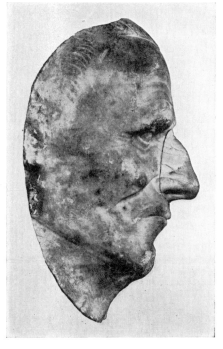

[b]

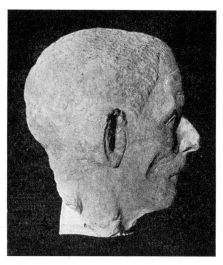

[c]

[*a*] STELE of AURELIUS HERMIA and his wife AURELIA. The figures are placed in a sunken panel. The woman's head, with veil, is restored; the man's thin and furrowed face is clearly that of a Roman of the last century of the Republic, and his draperies recall the *Aules Metilis* (48 [*d*]). The figures—the man's more especially— are strictly Italic in character, but they face one another in profile, clasping hands in an attitude that recalls the groups on Greek stelae, cf. the fine *lekythos* in Munich (H. Diepolder, *Die Attischen Grab-reliefs*, 1931, pl. 34). Found in 1593 in a tomb of the Via Nomentana *British Museum*. (ix, 813, 829.)

[*B.M. Cat. of Sculpture*, III, no. 2274; for the inscription and older history of the stele, see *C.I.L.* VI, 9499. *Photograph British Museum*]

[*b*] STELE of MAN AND WIFE (Palombino Marble). Height 1·81 m., width 0·4 m. The man wears the *toga exigua*. This and the coiffure of his wife induce A. Zadoks-Jitta to date the stele to about 90 B.C., while, from its style, Colini follows Horn in referring it to a some-what later date. Cf. Goethert, p. 50. (For details of the heads see 54 [*a*], [*b*].) Found in 1928 on the Via Statilia, not far from *Porta Maggiore*. *Rome, Museo Mussolini*. (ix, 813.)

[A. Zadoks-Jitta, p. 69; A. M. L. Colini, *Boll. Comm.* LIV, 1926, pp. 177 *sqq.*; R. Horn, *Stehende weibliche Gewandstatuen in der hellenistichen Plastik*, p. 81, Munich, 1931, p. 81. *Photograph German Institute*]

[*c*] STELE of VERGILIUS EURYSACES and ANTISTIA. The attribution of this stele to the tomb of the baker and contractor Vergilius Eurysaces outside the Porta Maggiore is almost certain. The stele, found near the tomb, and till recently walled up not far from it, has now been moved to the Terme. The figures are typical of the late Republican period, probably Caesarian. The woman's features are much rubbed and effaced; those of the man have late Republican death-mask character, sunken eyes, salient cheek-bones, etc.; the prominent forepart of the skull is another death-sign noted by Zadoks-Jitta. *Rome, Museo delle Terme*. (ix, 814.)

[A. Zadoks-Jitta, p. 55, O; E. C. Lovatelli, *Il Sepolcro di Eurisace* (*Passeggiate nella Roma Antica*, 1909), p. 160. *Photograph Carletti*]

[a]

[b]

[c]

[*a*] Obverse of a denarius issued by CN. BLASIO CN. F. *c.* 108 B.C. Portrait of Scipio Africanus the Elder. (*B.M. Cat. Roman Republic*, II, p. 296, 628.)

[*b*] Obverse of a denarius issued by MARCELLINUS *c.* 45 B.C. (?) Portrait of M. Claudius Marcellus, the Consul; a triskeles behind the head. (*Loc. cit.* I, p. 567, 4206.)

[*c*] Reverse of a denarius issued by Q. Pompeius Rufus *c.* 57 B.C. Portrait of Sulla. (*Loc. cit.* I, p. 484, 3883.)

[*d*] Obverse of a denarius issued by C. ANTIUS RESTIO *c.* 46 B.C. Portrait of the tribune Antius Restio. (*Loc. cit.* I, p. 521, 4030.)

[*e*] Engraved sard. Woman seated on ground, plant behind her, basket of fruit, two ants and ears of corn in front, bird holding sceptre above. (*B.M. Cat. Engraved Gems, etc.* p. 120, 1033; A. Furtwängler, *Antike Gemmen*, III, p. 293, fig. 154.)

[*f*] Obverse of a denarius issued by CALDUS *c.* 60 B.C. Portrait of the Consul C. Coelius Caldus. (*B.M. Cat. Roman Republic*, I, p. 474, 3833.)

[*g*] Obverse of a denarius issued by Q. Nasidius *c.* 36 B.C. Portrait of Pompey as Neptune, a dolphin below, a trident before the head. (*Loc. cit.* II, p. 564, 21.)

[*h*] Obverse of a denarius issued by TI. VET(urius Barrus?) *c.* 92 B.C. Bust of Mars. (*Loc. cit.* II, p. 281, 550.)

[*i*] Obverse of a denarius issued in 44 B.C. CAESAR as Dictator for life: his head laureate. (*Loc. cit.* I, p. 546, 4157.)

[*j*] Reverse of a denarius issued by M. SERVEILI(us). C. F. *c.* 89 B.C. Two horsemen dismounted and fighting on foot. (*Loc. cit.* I, p. 227, 1660.)

[*k*] Reverse of an aureus of *c.* 37 B.C. with a portrait of OCTAVIA. On the obverse (not shown) is a portrait of Antony. (*Loc. cit.* II, p. 507, 144.)

[*l*] Reverse of a denarius struck by T. DEID(us) *c.* 95 B.C. Deidius, Praetor in 138 B.C., armed with shield and whip striking down an armed Sicilian slave. (*Loc. cit.* II, p. 276, 530.)

[*j*] and [*l*] have been selected as showing what has been termed an Italic mode of composition in which the design appears to cut boldly into the background. (ix, 818.)

All enlarged 1½ diameters.

All in the *British Museum*.

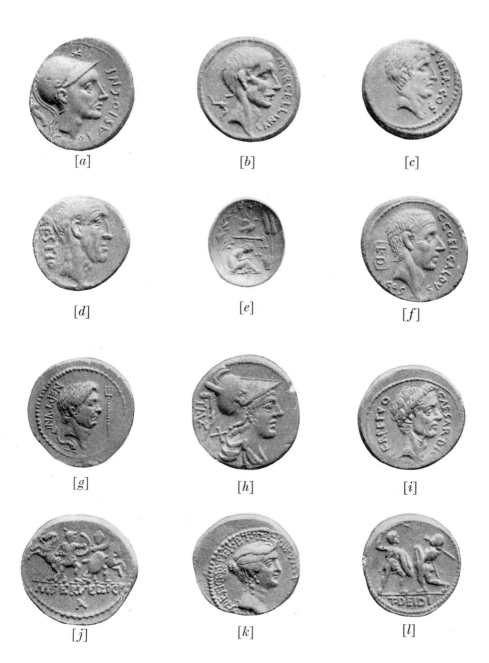

[a]   [b]   [c]

[d]   [e]   [f]

[g]   [h]   [i]

[j]   [k]   [l]

[*a*] ASH URN, with scene of ambush. The relief, which represents one of a series of episodes in the legend of the seer or prophet Cacus and his devotee Artile, has been well analysed by Messerschmidt, and traced by him to its Greek source. It is merely shown here to illustrate Italo-Etruscan composition, as analysed by Sieveking— the movement of the figures from back to front, and the way in which they are allowed to penetrate the background—a phenomenon to be observed in several reliefs of the same class. From *Città della Pieve. Florence, Museo Nazionale.* (ix, 818.)

[F. Messerschmidt, *J.D.A.I.* XLV, 1930, pp. 75 *sqq.*; J. Sieveking, *Das römische Relief, Festschrift f. Arndt*, p. 19 *sq.*, fig. 1; C. Robert, *Festschrift f. Blümel*, p. 75. *Photograph Alinari*]

[*b*] RELIEF: hunting scene; *c.* 50 B.C. Like the ash urn, this relief shows movement from back to front; see especially the horse rearing forward on the left, and the movement of the *putti* holding up the wreaths and appearing to dip right back into the background. The relief also shows how a composition deriving from Greek models could be transposed to an Italic mode by substituting the tri-dimensional Italic for the two-dimensional Greek principle. *Tomb* (S.W. side) *of the Julii, St Rémy in Provence.* (ix, 818.)

[J. Sieveking, *op. cit.* pp. 20 *sqq.*; E. Loewy, *Die Anfänge der Triumphbogen*, 1928, p. 24. *Photograph German Institute*]

[*c*] Detail of CISTA from PRAENESTE. Slaying of the Trojan Captives. From left to right; Achilles slays a Trojan prisoner at the foot of the funeral pyre of Patroclus; on the right another captive, naked and beardless like the first, stands with hands tied behind his back, looking sorrowfully at the scene; from the right a third, bearded captive is led by a Greek who averts his head; a second bearded and naked captive is led by a fully armed Greek. On the left of the picture (not illustrated here) are two more seated captives in attitudes of anguish. F. Messerschmidt has shown that this version of the myth is from a different source from that reproduced in the François Tomb. Here a section of the composition is re-produced to show the human and compassionate element introduced under Italic influence. *British Museum.* (ix, 818.)

[*B.M. Cat. of Bronzes*, 1899, p. 102, no. 638, pl. XXXI; F. Messerschmidt, *Probleme der etruskischen Malerei des Ilellenismus, J.D.A.I.* XLV, 1930.
  For greater clearness the illustration is taken from *B.M. Cat.*; F. Messerschmidt, *op. cit.* illustrates from photographs]

[a]

[b]

[c]

WALL-PAINTINGS from François tomb; *c.* mid fourth century B.C. For the plan of this tomb see 64.

[*a*] *Sacrifice of Trojan prisoners* (on left of central chamber or Tablunum, no. 12 in plan, p. 64). 3·25 m. × 1·70 m.

Each figure is inscribed with its name as follows: *a*, Agamemnon (*aχmenrun*); *b*, Patroclus (*hinθial patrocles*); *c*, Vanth (*vanθ*); *d*, Achilles (*aχle*); *e*, Trojan (*truials*); *f*, Charon (*χaru*); *g*, Ajax the Telamonian (*aivas tlamunus*); *h*, Trojan (*truials*); *i*, Ajax Oiliades (*aivas vilatas*); *j*, Trojan (*truials*). C.I. Etr. 5256 to 5265.

The last figure not illustrated.

In the centre, group of Achilles slaying a prisoner between Charon and Vanth, both intent on their duties as *psychopompi*. To the right, the two Ajax each with a prisoner; on the left, behind the Vanth, the ghost of Patroclus; on the extreme left, Agamemnon quietly surveys the scene, draped in his royal mantle. The broad sash round the breast of Patroclus is symbolic of violent death. The great round shield at his feet is presumably that of Achilles. Achilles wears a pale blue tunic with white stripes at the armholes. Though feeling the details are Etrusco-Italic, this is one of the closest interpretations extant of the great scene in *Iliad* XXIII.

[*b*] *The battle scene* (on right of central chamber of Tablunum, no. 9 on plan, p. 64). 3·12 × 1·66 m. Lower part damaged by damp.

Inscr.: *a*, caile vipinas (not in picture); *b*, macstrna; *c*, larθulθes; *d*, laris papaθnas velznaχ; *e*, pasna aecmsnas sveanaχ; *f*, rasce *g*, ven-icau xxx(x) plsaχs; *h*, avle vipinas. C.I. Etr. 5266 to 5273.

Three groups of combatants and two standing figures at end. The scene as explained by Messerschmidt is a surprise attack rather than a battle. It is evident that a number of bearded warriors (four in the picture) have attacked (see last group on the right) and fallen upon a group of unarmed beardless men, representing another clan (three in the picture), while on the left *Macstrna* is cutting the bonds of *caile vipinas*, brother of *aule vipinas* (on the right, dispatching the men whose armour is at his left). The composition in loosely connected groups of equal value is less pleasing than the compact centralization of the scene of the Trojan captives.

Discovered at *Vulci* in 1857, removed in 1862 to *Museo Torlonia, Rome.* For Bibliography see p. 64. Good copies of original size in Museo Gregoriano, Rome. (ix, 818, 820.) The subject of the release of Caile Vipinas also occurs on an urn in Chiusi (G. Körte, LII, 126, 8).

[Photographs L.U.C.E.]

[a]

[b]

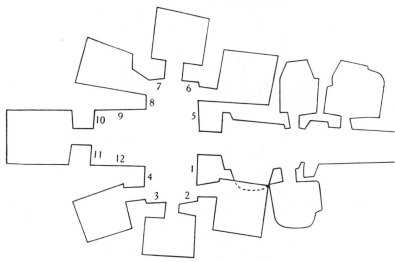

PLAN OF FRANÇOIS TOMB, VULCI,
after F. Messerschmidt and A. von Gerkan, p. 113

DETAILS OF WALL PAINTINGS

[a] Head of third Trojan prisoner, (j) from scene of Sacrifice not shown in illustrating facing p. 62 (no. 11 on plan).

[b] Head of *rasce*, (f) in battle scene, 62 [b].

[c] Head of *vel saties* (C.I. Etr. 5276) from the group of Vel Saties and his dwarf (no. 7 on plan). Shown to illustrate the introduction in certain of the paintings of an Hellenistic idealizing πάθos, in contrast to the simpler Italic naturalism. (ix, 818, 820.)

N.B. At no. 8 (on plan), round the corner and adjoining no. 9, is the group mentioned ix, 820; *marce camitlnas* (C.I. Etr. 5274) slaying *cneve tarχunies rujaχ* (5275). This is a distinct picture from no. 9 and of somewhat different proportions. We do not know for certain what episode is represented. Perhaps a copy after some contemporary picture.

[*Photographs German Institute*]
[F. Messerschmidt and A. von Gerkan, *Nekropole von Vulci*, 1930, pp. 62 *sqq.*, 140 *sqq.*, figs. 95, 96; F. Messerschmidt, *J.D.A.I.* xlv, 1940, p. 64, fig. 2; Helbig-Amelung, i, p. 321, no. 523; B. Nogara, figs. 225, 227; F. Poulsen, *Etruscan Tomb Paintings*, p. 54, fig. 39; see also A. Momigliano, *L' Opera dell Imperatore Claudio*, p. 33, n. 1. For their relation to Greek paintings see E. Pfuhl, *Malerei und Zeichnung der Griechen*, Munich, 1923, ii, 795; M. Rostovtzeff, *History of the Ancient World*, ii, pl. V; *C.A.H.* vii, pp. 388 *sqq.*]

[a]

[b]

[c]

[*a*] DETAILS FROM SARCOPHAGUS in tomb of the Volumni; third century B.C. The two winged figures (Lasai) adorn the angles of the base of the sarcophagus of Arnth Velimna in the innermost chamber of the Tomb of the Volumni. The *Lasai* sit with crossed legs and feet somewhat lifted from the ground, in carefully contrasted attitudes (right leg of the one figure raised to balance the left leg of the other figure, and so on); the heads, with their massive locks of hair, are modelled with singular force; short-sleeved undergarment open at the neck; heavy draperies drawn in at the waist into a belt; straps across the breast. The full effect of the figures as guardians of the tomb must have been even more powerful when the four figures painted within the central niche, as if peering from the underworld, were less effaced. In *Perugia*. (ix, 819.)

[A. Della Seta, *Monumenti dell Arte Antica Classica*, p. 133; P. Ducati, p. 567; B. Nogara, p. 279, figs, 153, 156]

[*b*] GROUP ON ASH URN. This rare subject, possibly made for a special occasion (death of a child, or of a young mother in giving it birth), represents in the centre the group of the mother seated with the child on her left arm. She turns round with a smile, clasping in her right hand the right hand of her husband, who enters from the left. It is a farewell scene, or has the man come to the underworld to join those he had lost? From the right, balancing the figure of the husband, Hades, wearing his skin helmet, enters from the gate of the underworld. On the extreme right is seated a kindly Charon, with his hammer in his hand, and shouldering his rudder. Above Charon a beast-headed guardian of the dead forms a pendant to a much mutilated figure in armour on the extreme left. In *Berlin*. (ix, 819.)

[F. Messerschmidt, *Röm, Mitt.* XLV, 1930, pp. 172 *sqq.*; G. Körte, 100, 16]

[*c*] TERRACOTTA GROUP of Athena and Heracles. Athena, helmeted, lays her left hand on the shoulder of Heracles, who is seated in front of her on a rock. His cloak, Athena's tunic and the base of the group are edged with a meander pattern. The thick feet and ankles are distinctively Italo-Etruscan (cf. 68 [*c*]). Since writing the description in the text the present writer (E.S.) has re-examined the terracotta and discovered that it is heavily restored; this is confirmed by letter from M. Michon who gives the restored details as follows: Of the Athena: head, right part of breast with Gorgoneion; right hand with jug and left arm. Of the Heracles: the head; right arm with patera, left hand and club. The group is from an antefix and part of the antique attachment to the tile end is extant. *Paris, Louvre.* (ix, 819.)

[W. Hausenstein, p. 53. *Photographs* [*a*], [*c*] *Alinari*; [*b*] *Staatliche Museen, Berlin*]

[c]

[a]

[b]

5-2

CISTAE AND TERRACOTTA

[*a*] CISTA from *Praeneste*; second half of fourth century B.C. The cista is of the well-known Praenestine type, with convex lid and two figures with arms extended and crossed forming the handle. The body is adorned with a scene of triumph; in the centre, facing, stand a general wearing a rich costume (tunic, long and sleeved, heavily embroidered hose), who holds the *patera* above a flaming tripod-alrat; in his left hand he grasps an eagle-topped sceptre; from the right advances a camillus with incense ladle and *urceus*, and a priest with veiled head; on the left side stands a triumphal chariot itself. In the careless Italic manner the feet are sometimes allowed to over-step the border on which the figures stand. *Berlin, Antiquarium.* (ix, 820.)

[*Berlin, Führer durch das Antiquarium*, p. 93, no. 6238, pl. 57. *Photograph Staatliche Museen, Berlin*]

[*b*] DETAIL FROM the Ficoroni *cista*. The figure of the Silenus beating his paunch is illustrated here as an instance of the intro-duction of Italic humour, and sense of broad fun, into a picture (an episode in the voyage of the Argonauts) borrowed, through with many modifications, from some Greek model. *Rome, Villa Guilia.* (ix, 821.)

[For the cista, see A. Della Seta, *Museo di Villa Giulia*, p. 481 (with bibl. and ill.). and *Italia Antica*, p. 295, fig. 330. Drawing after *Photograph Alinari*]

[*c*] TERRACOTTA ANTEFIX, Maenad and Satyr. One of a series of terracotta antefixes from a temple at *Satricum* (Conca), repre-senting the amorous encounter of a Maenad and Satyr. The variety of action and emotion, and the liveliness of the movements are equally admirable, though the legs and feet have the distinctive Italo-Etruscan thickness. *Rome, Villa Giulia.* (ix, 821.)

[A. Della Seta, *Museo di Villa Giulia*, pp. 262 *sqq.*, no. 10261 (with bibl. and ill.); E. Strong, *Art in Ancient Rome*, p. 114, fig. 124; E. Van Buren, *Figurative terracotta revetments in Etruria and Latium*, p. 24, pl. XV, fig. 1; H. Lehmann-Hartleben, *Antike Plastik (Festschrift Arndt)*, p. 118 (for the popularity of the subject on Italic soil); J. Heurgon, *Le Satyre at la Ménade Étrusques* (Mélanges, XLVI, 1929), p. 108, fig. 5. *Photograph Alinari*]

[b]

[a]

[c]

WALL-PAINTINGS from the Tomba Golini. The originals are now damaged beyond recognition; our illustrations are from the latest photographs of the copies in the Florence museum.

[a] Chopping wood, and getting ready the food ingredients.

[b] Preparing the food to the accompaniment of the flutes.

[c] The larder well stocked with beef, venison and poultry.

[d] In the kitchen.

All the figures are inscribed in Etruscan characters. *Orvieto.* (ix, 821.)

[G. C. Conesrabile, *Pitture murali scoperte in una necropoli presso Orvieto nel* 1863, de D. Golini, Florence 1865; cf. F. Poulsen, *Etruscan Tomb Paintings*, p. 40, fig. 33; M. H. Swindler, p. 253, fig. 424. Good reproductions of certain details (especially heads) in A. Solari, *Vita Pubblica e Privata degli Etruschi*, pl. XXI, fig. 37, pl. XXVI, fig. 49, pl. XLIX, figs. 96, 97, 98. *Photographs Alinari*]

[a]

[b]

[c]

[d]

RELIEFS from the tomb of the baker, *Vergilius Eurysaces*; c. 50 B.C. The friezes, which decorate the three remaining sides of the tomb, just below the cornice, represent the activities of a large bakery.

[*a*] 1. The process begins on the right; a slave empties the contents of a sack of grain (presumably just bought) into a receptacle, while one *togatus* (Vergilius himself?) superintends his work and four others negotiate the purchase at a table.

2. The grinding of the grain at two mills worked by asses (*molae asinariae*) and attended by two slaves.

3. The sifting of the flour in sieves at two tables. Between the tables a *togatus*, followed by a child with a purse, seems to argue with one of the slaves of the further table.

[*b*] 4. On the right another mill for refining the flour, or a kneading trough, worked this time by a horse (*mola iumentaria*).

5. The rolling and kneading of the dough by slaves at two tables between which stands a togate overseer.

6. The baking of the bread: a slave holds the bread in the oven in a long-handled pan.

[*c*] 7. On the left the loaves are carried by slaves to the large scales, weighed and packed in baskets in the presence of *togati*, and finally carried away by slaves to the purchasers.

For the monument see ix, 835 and 100, below. For the portraits see 52 [*c*]. *Rome, Porta Maggiore.* (ix, 822; x, 397.)

[E. C. Lovatelli, *Il Sepolcro di Eurisace, Passeggiate nella Roma Antica*, 1909, pp. 151 *sqq.*; M. Rostovtzeff, *Social and Economic History of the Roman Empire*, pl. IV (with descr. and bibl.); T. Warscher, *Art and Archaeology*, Oct. 1930, pp. 103 *sqq. Photographs Carletti*]

[a]

[b]

[c]

SAMNITE BRONZES

[*a*] BRONZE STATUETTE of Samnite warrior. He wears the full
Samnite accoutrement (cf. 78 [*a*] and [*c*]); bronze breast-plate
adorned with three bosses, greaves and a leather tunic. The helmet
almost certainly carried a high-plumed crest. For the breast-plate,
see two of exactly the same pattern in the Naples Museum (*Guida
Ruesch*, 1904, 1909) described by F. Weege, *Oskische Grabmalerei*,
J.D.A.I. xxiv, 3, 1909, p. 150, figs. 21, 22. Provenance uncertain.
Said to have been found in Sicily (which would be strange) 'ou dans
l'Italie Méridionale' (which is more likely). *Paris, Louvre.* (ix, 822.)

[A. de Ridder, *Bronzes Antiques du Mus. du Louvre*, no. 124, fig. 9, p. 47; M.
Rostovtzeff, *History of the Ancient World*, ii, pl. X (Rostovtzeff recognizes the
Samnite character of the armour). *Photograph Alinari*]

[*b*] BRONZE EQUESTRIAN STATUETTE. The warrior wears a
short chiton fastened at the waist by a belt; his helmet is engraved
with lotus-flowers. The ripple of the skin on the horse's haunches
indicated by fine parallel lines. The mane divided into strands
rendered in relief like the forelock. When less was known of Italico-
Greek art the bronze was held to be purely archaic Greek. Its
South-Italic character is now becoming evident. From *Grumentum*
in Lucania. *British Museum.* (ix, 823.)

[Forman Sale Catalogue (Sotheby's, June, 1899), no. 53; Burlington Fine Arts Club,
1903 (Cat. pls. 27 and 28); H. B. Walters, *Select Bronzes*, pl. 1 (these take the earlier
view that the bronze is archaic Greek); G. v. Lücken, *Ath. Mitt.* xliv, 1919, p. 67
(who compares the style to that of Chalcidian vases, while admitting that the horse
is not Chalcidian); W. Lamb, *Greek and Roman Bronzes*, p. 107 (where the non-Greek
or Italic character of the group was first pointed out). *Photograph British Museum*]

[a]

[b]

[a] Goddess, or dead woman with emblems of Persephone. The lady, clad in a long white garment, sits on a high-backed throne without arm-rests; in her raised hand she holds a blue flower, in her left a pomegranate—symbol at once of death and resurrection; another pomegranate is under the throne. On her head a small flat cap from which hangs a veil, round her neck a red necklace with pendant-drops. The chair has Ionic volutes. The type of the lady's face is non-Greek and purely Campanian. Found in 1814 in a tomb at *Nola* in Campania. *Berlin, Antiquarium.* (ix, 823.)

[After F. Weege, *Oskische Grabmalerei, J.D.A.I.* xxiv, 3, 1909, pl. 7, no. 3 and p. 102 *sq.* (with full description)]

[b] Goddess, or dead woman. The lady, enthroned and turned to the left, is looking at herself in a gilt mirror (note reflection of the features). Her long close-fitting tunic embroidered at the hem with a floral pattern surmounted by a ray-pattern in red. Over her tunic hangs a red mantle. Round her waist is a broad sash. Her left hand rests on the arm of her chair. In front of her stands a girl in a similar close tunic, embroidered down the front, with a ray-pattern round the bottom. She has no cloak. In her left hand is a tall basket overflowing with pomegranates. Other pomegranates in the field. The wall pattern of wavelines in this and the foregoing is characteristic of fourth- and third-century decoration. Found 1891 in a grave at *Cumae.* In *Naples.* (ix, 823.)

[Good coloured reproduction in *Mon. Linc.* i (Sogliano, p. 960), F. Weege, p. 100, no. 1]

[c], [d] These two details from the Villa dei Misteri at *Pompeii* (see viii, 697 and *Volume of Plates* iii, 174) are shown here to illustrate the Campanian type of the faces. (ix, 823.)

[*Photographs Alinari*]

[a]

[b]

[d]

[c]

[a] Mounted horseman in full Samnite panoply. Fourth or early third century B.C. Found in *Sta. Maria di Capua*, painted on the narrow wall of a tomb. Fully described in the text. *Capua, Museo Campano.* (ix, 824.) See also F. Weege, p. 103, no. 6.

[b] Horse and groom. A young man, wearing a short red tunic and short yellow cloak, holds a horse by the bridle; in his left hand a whip. From *Gnazia* (Egnatia). In *Naples, Museo Nazionale.* (ix, 824.)

[F. Weege, p. 126, no. 49. *Photograph Alinari*]

[c] Group of Samnite warriors. On the left a woman offers the cup of welcome or departure to a warrior clad in the Samnite accoutrement and carrying a flag; behind him a squire holds his shield; behind him again is a mounted warrior followed by a squire or servant in a white tunic. The painting is framed at the top by a double key-pattern and at the bottom by a wave-pattern. Dated by Weege to the early fourth century, but perhaps later. Found at *Paestum.* In *Naples, Museo Nazionale.* (ix, 824.)

[V. Spinazzola, p. 3; M. H. Swindler, fig. 436; F. Weege, p. 116, no. 30 (full description and bibliography). *Photograph Alinari*]

[a]

[b]

[c]

[*a*] SUNK PANEL, with relief interpreted as Mettius Curtius leaping full-armed into the chasm in the Forum. The motive of rider and horse reappears not infrequently on Roman lamps; according to Couissin the rider, both on the lamps and on this relief, is clearly Samnite in origin. For the slab inscribed *Lucius Naevius Surdinus*, on the back of which the relief is carved, see *B.S.R. Cat.* (cited below), where the various views as to its dating are discussed, and also the place it possibly occupied, on a balustrade round the Lacus Curtius. The relief has long been regarded as only a copy, but with greater knowledge of Italic work, it would seem to be an original of the first century B.C. For the date accepted in the text see C. C. Van Essen, *Chronologie*, p. 46 *ss.* and p. 59 note. *Rome, Museo Musqolini.* (ix, 824.)

[Originally on the staircase of the Conservatori. *B.S.R. Cat. of the Palazzo dei Conservatori*, p. 37, pl. 13; P. Couissin, *Rev. Arch.* 1930, pp. 265, 269, 278. Å. Åkerström, 'Lacus Curtius und seine Sagen', in *Corolla Archeologica*, Lund, 1932, pp. 72 *sqq*. *Photograph German Institute*]

[*b*] WALL-PAINTING: two gladiators fighting. The gladiators are wearing short tunics striped with blue and red; the neck and arm-holes are edged with red, and the girdles are yellow; the round shields are yellow (bronze) edged with leather, and with a red boss; the greaves come to above the knee, but no protection is given to the thighs, which are pierced with wounds. One spear is stuck in the left-hand man's shield, and another in the thigh of the right-hand man, who continues to fight with animation, though his drawn face and compressed lips betray his agony. *Capua, Museo Campano.* (ix, 824.)

[F. Weege, pl. XI, no. 14]

[*c*] WALL-PAINTING: dancing women. Third century B.C. (?). Five women with one man as leader, linked in the dance; part of a frieze decorating a tomb. Rich colouring, in which white, black, red, yellow and blue are employed. From *Ruvo* in Apulia. In *Naples, Museo Nazionale.* (ix, 824.)

[V. Spinazzola, p. 81 (with description)]

[a]

[b]

[c]

ROMAN WALL-PAINTING

[*a*] WALL-PAINTING. This wall-painting belongs to the earlier phase of the second or architectural style of Pompeian painting, when architectural features were simply combined with the panel decoration of the first style, without the introduction of any pictorial element. The painting adorns a room with elegant mosaic pavement (in the centre, within a square, a chessboard decoration in *opus sectile*) which belongs to a very fine house of Republican date under the *lararium* of the Flavian Palace. A long podium, decorated, like the centre of the floor, with a chessboard pattern, has projecting bases at regular intervals to support the pillars that enframe panels painted in imitation of marble. *Rome, Palatine.* (ix, 827.)

[G. E. Rizzo, *La Pittura Ellenistico-Romana*, pl. IV, p. 7; cf. G. Lugli, *Monumenti Antichi di Roma*, 2nd ed. 1931, p. 304. *Photograph lent by Prof. G. E. Rizzo*]

[*b*] DETAIL of WALL-PAINTING. Section from the famous 'white room' in the 'House of Livia' (perhaps the house of Hortensius, and anyhow of Republican date). Though the swags of fruit and flowers are often said to be imitated from the *Ara Pacis*, they probably belong to the same school of floral decoration, which began earlier than Augustus. The swags are most skilfully suspended behind the painted column, thus emphasizing the feeling of space between this and the white panels that adorn the actual wall. Above the panels runs the yellow monochrome frieze. (For this frieze see M. Rostovtzeff, *Hellenistisch-römische Architekturlandschaft, Röm. Mitt.* 1911, 1–2.) *Rome, Palatine.* (ix, 828.)

[After L. Curtius, *Die Wandmalerei Pompejis*, p. 90, pl. 54]

[a]

[b]

ROUND BASE for a trophy or statue. Height 0·528 m.; Diameter 0·548 m. below, 0·434 m. above. The base tapers slightly towards the top. Its frieze represents, according to the most recent interpretation (Goethert), a sacrifice in honour of Hercules Victor. In the centre an altar whose mouldings recall those of the altar on the frieze of Domitius Ahenobarbus (86 [*b*]). To the left of the altar Hercules with club and lion-skin, possibly the central figure to whom the sacrifice is offered (cf. Mars on the Domitius altar). The draped male figure in front of Hercules must be a *fidicen*, or lyre-player, not Apollo (the same figure occurs on the Domitius frieze). Behind the altar two flute-players (*tibicines*). In the front plane, advancing towards the altar from the right, the procession of the *suovetaurilia* (note frontal movement of the assistants). To the right again, a goddess with sceptre, interpreted by C. Weickert as Venus Genetrix, from which, however, it differs in type, being more probably, as F. W. Goethert points out, Iuventas, accompanied by a winged Victory. *Rome, Villa Borghese.* (ix, 829.)

[C. Weickert, *Ein römisches Relief aus der Zeit Caesars*, Festschrift Arndt, pp. 48 *sqq.*; F. W. Goethert, p. 18. *Photographs German Institute*]

[a]

[b]

[c]

[d]

[*a*] RELIEF with gladiators; Italic marble (Luna?). Height 0·59 m., Breadth (above) 1·075 m. C. Weickert, who first drew attention to this frieze, dated it to the Sullan period (*c*. 90–80 B.C.), but this date seems much too early, as has recently been shown. The accoutrement of the gladiators is found as late as the Imperial period, and tells little for the dating. F. W. Goethert has shown that the harsh folds of the drapery of the trumpeter recall the base of Civita Castellana. The spare elongated forms, from which all superfluous flesh seems to have been banished, take us a long way from the round fleshiness of most of the figures on the Domitius frieze or the Borghese base. The relief is described in the text. *Munich, Glyptothek.* (ix, 830.)

[C. Weickert. *Gladiatoren-relief der Münchner Glyptothek, Münchner Jahrbuch,* N.F. II, 1/2; and F. W. Goethert, p. 51. *Photograph lent by Professor Weickert*]

[*b*], [*c*] CIRCULAR ALTAR or BASE; Italic marble. Height 1·04 m., Height of relief 0·85 m., Diameter 0·70 m. A triad of divinities— Venus Genetrix between Mars (r.) and Vulcan (l.). Immediately behind Mars an altar piled with fruit, at which a bearded Roman general is pouring libation, followed by a Victory who holds up a wreath with her right hand. The faces much rubbed. The frieze is interrupted at the back, where a *boukranion* corresponds to the figure of Mars in front. The beard of the general, unusual in the first century, suggests an historical or legendary character (Aeneas?, Romulus?). Owing to the presence of Venus Genetrix it cannot be dated earlier than the year of the dedication of the *cultus* image in the temple vowed to her by Caesar, 46 B.C. It is rightly dated by R. Herbig to *c*. 40 B.C., and he, like F. W. Goethert, brings it into connection with the gladiatorial relief at Munich.

Probably a base supporting a trophy, similar to the one carried by Mars. *Civita Castellana, Cathedral.* (ix, 829.)

[R. Herbig, *Röm. Mitt.* XLII, 1927, pls. 15–18 and pp. 129–47, with reff.; F. W. Goethert, p. 28. *Photographs German Institute*]

[a]

[b]

[c]

[*a*] Part of the SUBSTRUCTURE WALL inside the podium of the temple of Jupiter Capitolinus; tufa. *Rome, Museo Mussolini.* (ix, 832.)

[Platner-Ashby, p. 297. s.v. *Jupiter Optimus Maximus Capitolinus Aedes. Photograph Governatorato*]

[*b, c*] SUBTERRANEAN FOUNDATIONS (*fundationes*, Vitruv., III, 4, 1) of the sixth-century temple (Juno Regina?) on the Acropolis of *Ardea.* (ix, 832.)

[A. Sestini and A. Boethius, *Studii Mediterranei,* I, 1, Pl. II; *ib.* II, 2; A. Boethius, *Roma,* 1934, pp. 291 *sqq. Photographs given by Prof. A. Boethius, the excavator of Ardea*]

[a]

[b]

[c]

[*a*] TEMPLE A of the *area sacra* at the Largo Argentina in Rome, showing the two apses of the church of S. Nicola del Calcarario later built into it. The temple was hexastyle and peripteral, with nine columns on each side. It was of tufa coated with stucco; the Italian podium has severely-cut elegant mouldings; the broad flight of stairs in the front is of peperino. See plan, vol. ix, facing p. 829.

[*b*] TEMPLE B of the Largo Argentina, showing a first temple with sixteen columns, afterwards enlarged by walling up the inter-columnal spaces and bringing the columns into the interior; a new podium with slanting slabs to drain off the water falling from the roof was then added. The whole is of tufa, once coated with stucco. The temple is more usually identified as that of Hercules Custos; though G. Marchetti-Longhi proposes to see in it the Temple of Juno Regina; he believes that the huge statue basement within the temple was for a colossal acrolithic statue which he thinks to be of Juno, and of which the marble head and extremities (with exception of left arm) were found between Temples B and C. L. Du Jardin, on the other hand, believes the head to represent Apollo (*crinitus*) and to have been the cult-statue of the archaic Temple C. However this may be, Du Jardin makes a fairly good case for the existence in Rome of a third Temple of Apollo besides the Sosianus and the Palatinus. (ix, 833.)

[G. Marchetti-Longhi, *L' Area Sacra ed i templi repubblicani del Largo Argentina*, 1930, pp. 45 *sqq.*
L. Du Jardin, 'Monumenti antichi dell' area di S. Nicola ai Cesarini' in *Rend. Pont. Accad. Rom. Archeol.* vol. VIII, 1932.
G. Marchetti-Longhi, 'Il colossale Simulacro marmoreo rinvenuto al Largo Argentina' in *Boll. dell' Assoc. Internaz, Studi Mediterr.*, Anno III, 1933. B. Wijkström, 'Welche sind die Tempel auf der Piazza Argentina,' in *Corolla Archeologica*, Lund, 1932, pp. 17 *sqq. Photographs Anderson*]

[a]

[b]

[*a*] Part of the SARCOPHAGUS of L. CORNELIUS SCIPIO BARBATUS, consul in 298 B.C. (*C.I.L.* I, 6–7 for the inscription in Saturnian Verse). It is of peperino and is shaped like an oblong altar. Along the top runs a Doric frieze of triglyphs and metopes adorned with rosettes of varied shapes; above a row of dentils; the lid is adorned with large Ionic volutes. The sarcophagus was found in the Sepulchre of the Scipios on the left of the Via Appia in 1780 and removed to the *Vatican.* (ix, 834.)

[Helbig³, I, p. 7, no. 125. W. Amelung, *Sculpturen des Vat. Mus.* I. *Photograph Anderson*]

[*b*] *Praeneste.* TEMPLE of FORTUNA. Part of the podium of the large hall usually identified as the actual shrine. The podium has a lower moulding; above runs a Doric frieze similar to that of the Scipio sarcophagus, with charmingly decorated paterae introduced among the rosettes above an egg moulding and above again a row of dentils. The elements of this type of decoration were Hellenic, but became Italic in application; we find them above the Arco di Augusto at Perigua (first century B.C.) where the rosettes are replaced with apotropaic significance by round shields. The podium supports half columns on low plinths, a scheme afterwards imitated in wall decorations of the second style. In the text attention is called to the delicacy of the carving, yet this lacks the accuracy and sharpness of the ornament of the sarcophagus. (ix, 834, 839.)

[R. Delbrück, *Hellenistische Bauten in Latium*, I, p. 85 f. *Photograph Alinari*]

[b]

[a]

7-2

TOMB OF THE BAKER

TOMB OF THE BAKER M. VERGILIUS EURYSACES (for the construction see ix, 835); the inscription, repeated, with variants in the spelling, on each side of the monument, reads:

Est hoc monimentum Marcei Vergilei Eurysacis, pistoris, redemptoris, apparet (*C.I.L.* i, 1013–15).

The frieze with the baking operations has been described above, p. 72. The sepulchral slab from the front of the tomb (p. 52 [c] above), with the portraits of the baker and his wife Antistia, has recently been moved to the Museo delle Terme—and it is proposed to clear the whole area round the tomb, down to the level of its original pavement. (ix, 814; 822, 830, 835.)

[Platner-Ashby, p. 479 *s.v. sepulcrum Eurysacis.* Dessau 7460a–c. For bibliography see p. 72 above. *Photograph Carletti*]

EST HOC MONIMENTVM MARCI VERGILEI EVRYSAC

[a] DORIC TEMPLE at *Cori*, said, without evidence, to have been consecrated to Hercules. The inscription (*C.I.L.* I, 1149; x, 6517) on the door lintel of the cella reads:

M · M · ELIVS · M · F · L · TVRPILIVS · L · F · DVOMVIRES · DE ·
SENATVS SEN*tent* · IA · AEDEM · FACIENDAM · COERAVERVNT ·
EISDEMQVE · PROBAVERE

The temple had four broadly spaced columns in the front, and a deep vestibule. The podium is much damaged, but, according to Delbrück's calculations, it was low with a broad flight of steps in the front. The breadth of the cella apparently exceeded its depth.
[R. Delbrück, *op. cit.* II, pp. 23–36, with plans and a detailed description]

[b] Two remaining columns of a CORINTHIAN TEMPLE at *Cori* (ancient Cora) dedicated to the Castores (*C.I.L.* x, 6506). The temple is in pure Italic plan and of Republican character, but, from the lighter foliation of the Corinthian capitals, perhaps later than Sulla.
[See Hülsen in P.W. *s.v. Cora. Photographs Alinari*]

[c] The TWO TEMPLES at *Tivoli*, above the cascades: on the left the round temple with its ring of columns (originally eighteen in number), on high podium, commonly thought, but without evidence, to be that of Vesta: for the remains of a dedicatory inscription see *C.I.L.* XIV, 3573. On the right the pseudoperipteral rectangular temple, seen from the back. It had a cella *in antis*, four columns in the front and a flight of steps. (ix, 838.)
R. Delbrück, *op. cit.* II, pp. 11–22 (with plans, etc.). *Photograph Dr Ashby*]

[a]

[b]

[c]

[*a*] TEMPLE OF JUPPITER at *Pompeii*, showing the Italic podium, deep colonnaded vestibule with six columns and broad flight of fifteen steps on the front. The columns, which were of the Corinthian order (one capital remains), are of tufa coated with stucco. The cella is about half the length of the whole temple, but is not tripartite. (ix, 838.)

[*Photograph Alinari*]

[*b*] Detail from the interior of the TABULARIUM, *Rome*: the large room in magnificent *opus quadratum* forming vestibule to the lower floor of the tabularium, with the stairs that lead to the subterranean gallery. (ix, 840.)

[See G. Lugli, *La Zona Archeologica di Roma*², pp. 36 *sqq*. *Photograph Dr Lugli*]

[a]

[b]

TEMPLE OF ANXUR at *Terracina*: [*a*] Western side of the huge arcaded substructures in Sullan *opus incertum*.
[*Photograph Dr Ashby*]

[*b*] Inner arcades of the front of the substructures of the same temple in Sullan *opus incertum*. (ix, 839.)
[G. Lugli, *Forma Urbis Italiae*, 1926, p. 166 (V zone, fig. 13). *Photograph Dr Lugli*]

Praeneste. General view of the whole SANCTURY OF FORTUNA, restored, with its temples and terraces. (ix, 839.)

[H. C. Bradshaw, *Papers of the British School at Rome*, vol. IX, pl. XXXIII]

[a] AUGUSTUS AND HIS SUITE. Restorations: none. The slab is put together out of a number of fragments. The figure of Augustus of which little is preserved was carved on two blocks. In the centre Augustus, represented taller than the rest and wearing wreath and veil, is shown in three-quarter view to the left. Part of his right arm is preserved and from its movement it would seem that the Emperor was offering libation at an altar, which however must have been of small dimensions. The head covering differs from that of other personages of the frieze who are *capite velato*, in consisting apparently of a separate piece of stuff lighter than the drapery. Facing Augustus a figure wearing the festal wreath; on the left a group of lictors (fragmentary). Behind the Emperor, lower part of a camillus (fragments of legs, tunic and of the fringed cloth or *mappa*). On the right, fragments of a figure wearing the wreath and of a group of four lictors. It is uncertain whether Augustus appears here as Pontifex Maximus, an office he took over in 12 B.C. (in which case another interpretation must be found for the tall figure of the priestly group possibly representing Lepidus (see 114 [a]), or as *rex sacrorum* (according to Petersen and Sieveking), though there is no record of Augustus filling this office, or more simply, as Paribeni the latest interpreter of the relief suggests, as *princeps senatus* and *pater patriae* with the head veiled as was the custom at every libation or *nuncupatio votorum* (cf. the veiling of the *paterfamilias* who preformed a ritual act). These are problems, like others connected with the friezes of the Ara Pacis, which may be more clearly resolved when the excavation under the Palazzo Fiano is completed and all the pieces of the frieze are put together and re-examined. Found in the excavations of 1903. *Rome, Museo delle Terme* (x, 479, 546 *sqq.*). For the ground-plan of the altar see x, Plan facing p. 582.

[b] Detail, HEAD OF AUGUSTUS, showing the likeness to his best accredited portraits.

[General Bibliography to Ara Pacis: R. Paribeni, *Museo Naz. Romano*, no. 102 (with older bibliography); see also E. Strong, *Scultura Romana*, pp. 19 *sqq.*; E. Rizzo, *Capitolium*, II, 1926, p. 457; A. Colini in *Enciclop. Italiana s.v.* Ara Pacis Augustae. For the Augustus slab as now put together, see R. Paribeni, *Boll. d' Arte*, 1931, pp. 3 *sqq. Photographs Museo delle Terme*]

[a]

[b]

SLAB with the imperial family (south side). Restored: the whole lower part of the slab with feet; all noses; head and hands of the elder boy, hands of the girl. From left to right, group of four figures; a young woman holding a small boy, doubtless her child, by the hand and turning back towards a young man in military dress, probably her husband. In the background between them a veiled woman lifts her left forefinger to her mouth as if enjoining silence upon the young couple. From the fact that he does not wear the toga like the other male personages of the procession, but military dress with *paludamentum*, the man is often identified with Nero Drusus, at the time commander of the forces in Germany. The lady in front of him must then be Antonia Minor, the child Germanicus. The group is harmonious, and self-contained, though linked with the following group of six persons by the boy who grasps the cloak of the supposed Drusus. The next group is more loosely compacted. The young man is generally identified as Domitius Ahenobarbus with his wife Antonia Maior and their two children: a girl who smiles protectively at the little brother (?), who holds on to the cloak of Drusus while his mother places a guiding hand on his right shoulder. The little girl, whose hair is gathered in a bun at the nape, wears long undertunic and mantle and a necklet with crescent-shaped pendant. In the background a young woman walks or stands in front of Antonia; then comes an elderly man and in the extreme right half concealed by the figure of Domitius a young man with fine sculpturesque head. In *Florence, Uffizi*. (x, 479, 547.) For Bibliography see 112.

[*Photograph German Institute*]

[a] TERRA MATER, central detail from panel of ARA PACIS, in *Florence*. Very heavily restored and worked over; for details see E. Petersen, *Ara Pacis Augustae*, p. 49. The notion that the Terra Mater slab does not belong to the Ara Pacis (cf. Rostovtzeff, *Bulletin des Antiquaires de France*, 1925, p. 209) is not tenable, as pilasters on either side of the slab seem identical with others on the balustrade. Tellus, or Terra Mater, is seated on a rock surrounded by emblems of fertility: children on her lap; in the background poppyheads, ears of corn, and reeds. Below, a cow resting and a sheep drinking. The absence of the cornucopiae is compensated for by fruits and corn. As a rule Terra Mater reclines in contact with her element, though there are examples to the contrary (*e.g.* 150, 156 [a]). On either side are allegorical figures (not illustrated): one on the right riding a sea-monster, the other a swan, and interpreted as breezes (the *Jovis aurae* of Horace, *Carm. Saec.* 29 *sq.*) or more probably as air and water. The central figure has also been interpreted as Italia (*Saturnia tellus*, Virgil, *Georg.* II, 136 *sqq.*). But while Tellus is familiar throughout imperial art, there is no known effigy of Italia between the coin of *c.* 55 B.C. (see Mattingly in *J.R.S.* XII, 1922, p. 236) and Nerva (A.D. 96–8), when she reappears as protectress of the *proles Italica*, shown as children at her side, carrying a cornucopiae, and standing (or kneeling before the Emperor) but never sitting. The Italia of Antonine coins seated on the globe as 'sovereign country of the Roman world' (Toynbee, *The Hadrianic School*, p. 116) has no connection. The *Pax Augusta* of 13 B.C. brought prosperity and peace to the whole *Orbis*; to replace Terra Mater (=Orbis Terrarum, see 150) by Italia would narrow down an imperial conception to one of local significance and would rob the four entrance slabs of their climax. Nor does Italia seem invested with a sufficient religious importance to balance the Roma of the Ara. No cult or temple of Italia is known, whereas Tellus or Terra Mater had a temple and ancient ritual. Supporters of the Italia theory have however overlooked one argument. Possibly the *Italia in pariete picta* in the Temple of Tellus (Varro, *de Re Rust.* II) was a picture (not a map as suggested in *Art in Anc. Rome*, I, p. 60): if so there would be, as Prof. Lehmann-Hartleben points out to the writer, a precedent for an Italia on the Ara Pacis, showing a connection between Italia and Tellus. (x, 464, 479, 548.)

[For general bibliography see p. 112. For Italia: W. van Buren, *J.R.S.* III, 1913, pp. 134 *sqq.*; A. Grenier, *Le Génie Romain*, pp. 420 *sqq.*; L. R. Taylor, *The Divinity of the Roman Emperor*, p. 197. For Terra Mater: L. Curtius, *Sitzber. Heidelb. Akad.* 1923, 4, p. 11; E. Loewy, *Atti del I. Congresso di Studi Romani*, 1928, pp. 1 *sqq.*; G. Méautis, *Bronzes ant. du Canton de Neufchâtel* (Univ. de Neufchâtel), 1928, pp. 17 *sqq.*; F. Altheim, *Terra Mater*, in *Religionsgesch. Versuche und Vorarbeiten*, XXII, 1930, p. 121; E. Strong, *Scultura Romana*, I, p. 20. *Photograph German Institute*]

[b] SLAB from CARTHAGE, central group, in the *Louvre*. Free replica of 120 [a], unrestored, and presumably inspired by the same model. The allegories on either side (not illustrated) are different and have been interpreted as Sun and Moon. The debated question of style and priority cannot be settled until the prototype is discovered. Hellenistic character is usually claimed for this relief while 120 [a] is regarded as a Roman transformation. (x, 548, 552.)

[For Bibliography see p. 112; and G. Méautis, *op. cit.* p. 17 *sq. Photograph Alinari*]

[a]

[b]

[*a*] Panel with SACRIFICE OF AENEAS (west side). Restorations: none. The panel is broken at either end and along the top and the lower edges. Aeneas, a tall bearded figure, *capite velato*, offers sacrifice at a garlanded rustic altar. Behind him leaning on his spear stands *fidus Achates* (right shoulder with spear and right arm only preserved), while from the left advances a camillus with fruit-laden *patera* and jug, followed by a second camillus who drives the sow forward from a cave. Though the litter of thirty young is absent this is evidently the sacrifice on the spot where Aeneas saw the prodigy of the sow (Virgil, *Aen.* III, 383 *sqq.*). Above the cave appears a little shrine within which sit the *Penates* (x, 548), whose cult had been restored by Augustus, Aeneas here bearing the double character of Aeneas the ancestor and of Aeneas-Augustus. On the Ara this panel is thought to have faced that of the Lupercal.

[*Photograph Alinari*]

[*b*] Detail from the lower outer frieze. Upper part of a great acanthus stem branching out to right and left into foliated spirals ending in flowers or else in bunches of leaves. Between the two main stems springs a third and slighter stem supporting a swan with curving neck, generally interpreted as the swan of Apollo, whose cult was dear to Augustus, though it might also be the swan of the ancestral Venus Genetrix.

Both in *Rome, Museo delle Terme*. For bibliography see p. 112. (x, 479, 550.)

[*Photograph German Institute*]

[a]

[b]

RELIEFS

[*a*] Detail from the inner frieze of ARA PACIS. Restorations: none. Rich garland of flowers, fruit and foliage suspended by means of fluttering ribbons from a *bucranium* or ox skull. In the empty space a patera decorated with *umbilicus* and pattern of rays and leaves. In *Rome, Museo delle Terme.*

[*Photograph Alinari*]

[*b*] Panel from an altar. Restorations: none. The panel is adorned by two crossing cornuacopiae ending in capricorn heads. The grapes, the vine leaves, the pine-cone, the bird pecking at the fruit and the capricorn heads are all treated with a clarity and harshness of outline which recall Republican art, so that the relief is datable to about the period of the Second Triumvirate. The crossing cornua-copiae with capricorn heads are also found on the front of an altar in Bologna of later date, representing a liberation in honour of Augustus Hermes (?), where they are accompanied by the *caduceus*, symbol of peace and plenty. For the origin and symbolism of op-posing or crossing cornuacopiae, see Lehmann-Hartleben, *op. cit.* p. 165 and W. W. Tarn in *J.R.S.* XXII, 1932, p. 137; cf. also the four point to point cornuacopiae, 158 [*b*]. Crossing cornuacopiae occur on coins inscribed *Euthenia* (= *Abundantia*) quoted by Waser in P. W. *s.v.* Euthenia, col. 1500; on an altar (M. L. Deubner, *Röm. Mitt.* XLV, 1930, pp. 37 *sqq.*; and on glass pastes (A. Furtwängler, *Beschr. geschnitt. Steine in Berlin*, 1896, 6131, 6178 *sq.*; p. 224 *sq.*), which have also the capricorn motive. The capricorn must contain a reference to Augustus, direct or indirect. On the altars the crossed cornuacopiae may be the emblem of a *sodalitas.* Found in *Rome* on Via Salaria near Villa Savoia; therefore possibly from a tomb. In *Rome, Museo delle Terme.*

[K. Lehmann-Hartleben, *Röm. Mitt.* XLII, 1927, p. 167, pl. 21. *Photograph German Institute*]

[*c*] The SARCOPHAGUS CAFFARELLI. Restorations: none. The front part of the sarcophagus is adorned with two swags of flowers and fruit hanging by jeans of *taeniae* from *bucrania.* In the field a sacrificial jug or *urceus*, and a *patera* with the usual ray pattern. The naturalistic treatment of the flowers contrasts with the rich pulplike rendering of fruit and of flower petals on the Ara Pacis. Rodenwaldt dates the sarcophagus to the Tiberian period and com-pares its garlands to those of an altar in Naples dedicated in A.D. 18. But the treatment of the garlands on this *ara* comes closer in style to the Ara Pacis, so that the sarcophagus might be as late as the Claudian period. From the shape and from the fact that the back of the sarcophagus is also carved, Rodenwaldt supposes a Greek workshop, but the ornament is indubitably Roman. In *Berlin.* (x, 550.)

[G. Rodenwaldt, *Berl. Winckelmanns Progr.* 82, 1925; J. H. Toynbee, *J.R.S.* XVII, 1927, p. 18. *Photograph Berlin Museum*]

[a]   [b]

[c]

[a] RELIGIOUS CEREMONY on a Della Valle-Medici relief. Restored: central part, left side; for details of restorations see Petersen, *Ara Pacis*, p. 90. The reconstruction of the slab in the façade of Villa Medici is full of uncertainties. The youthful figure wearing the priestly cap is from the features evidently a Julio-Claudian prince. On his right was presumably an altar at which he was offering libation. Immediately behind the young prince is an officer of state and in the background a group of lictors. At some distance in front of him walks a camillus wearing the festal wreath and *torques* and holding one of the imperial *lares*. A group of citizens on the left are looking on. It seems certain that the officiant is the youthful Claudius, so that the ceremony may be connected with the augurship bestowed on him in A.D. 8 when he was 18. From considerations of style the date suggested in vol. x (553) now appears to the present writer to be still too early; the frieze might be Claudian and come from some monument (one of the two *arcus Britannici* for instance; cf. x, 582 and 190 [*a, b*] below) in which Claudius as Emperor glorified the few salient events of his inglorious youth. Already in A.D. 6 assigned a part with Germanicus in the *ludi gladiatorii* in honour of his father Nero Drusus (Dio LV, 27), he was *augur* in A.D. 8 (*C.I.L.* III, 381; v, 24; Suet. *Claud.* 4); in the same or the previous year honoured by a statue on the arch at Pavia with other members of the Julian family (*C.I.L.* v, 6416, 10); *Augustales*, A.D. 14 (*C.I.L.* III, 381; Tac. *Ann.* I, 54; Suet. *ib.* 6); *Sodales Titii* (*C.I.L. ib.*); chosen *patronus* by *equites*, A.D. 14 and 31; chief mourner at the funeral of Germanicus, A.D. 20 (Tac. *Ann.* III, 2, 3); senator and consul under Gaius, A.D. 41. It should also be noted that the *Ara Pietatis Augustae* to which the Della Valle friezes are sometimes attributed had been completed by Claudius in A.D. 43 and probably decorated by him (*C.I.L.* VI, 562 and cf. Platner-Ashby, p. 390).

[b] SACRIFICIAL SCENE from the same frieze. Restored: all the architecture, the altar and the figures on left. The fine and carefully studied motive of the bull, originally perhaps inspired by a Greek model, is rendered here with a force and freedom that are almost Flavian.

Both in *Rome, Villa Medici* (formerly in the Della Valle Collection). (x, 553.)

[J. Sieveking, *Oest. Jahresh.* 1907, 190; *Rom. Sculpt.* p. 68; O. Brendel, *Röm. Mitt.* XLV, 1930, p. 201 and p. 204 (for the sacrifice). *Photographs German Institute*]

[a]

[b]

[*a*] SILVER CUP with Augustus as world ruler. The Emperor holding the globe as symbol of world dominion sits enthroned in three-quarter view. On his right he receives gifts from the gods of the State: Livia (?) as Venus Genetrix accompanied by a winged Cupid presents a statuette of Victoria as if to place it on the globe (*Victoria Augusti*). Behind her follows the Genius Populi Romani holding a cornucopiae and Roma in amazon panoply. On the Emperor's left the god Mars in full military dress introduces a group of figures personifying the provinces of the empire with Africa wearing the elephant hide at their head. On the reverse (not illustrated): Augustus seated on the *sella curulis* receives the submission of the conquered peoples. Found at *Boscoreale*. In *Coll. Edmond de Rothschild, Paris.*

[*b*] SILVER CUP with triumph of Tiberius. Tiberius, holding sceptre and palm branch, stands in the chariot while a figure behind him places the laurel wreath upon his head. An escort follows the imperial quadriga. Reverse (not illustrated), sacrificial scene at the temple of Juppiter Capitolinus. The advanced style of the relief and the sense of tridimensional depth shown in the arrangement of the figures on both cups suggest a late, perhaps Claudian, date. From the subjects—submission of the *orbis* to Augustus and triumph of Tiberius (variously referred to the triumph over the Sugambri in 7 B.C. or to the triumph over the Pannonians in A.D. 12)—it is probable that some sculptural or pictorial composition of Augustan date was reproduced in a later style. Companion to the Augustus cup. Found at *Boscoreale*. In *Coll. Edmond de Rothschild, Paris.* (x, 553, 609.)

[H. de Villefosse, *Mon. Piot*, v, 1899, pp. 31 *sqq.*; E. Strong, *Scultura Romana*, I, figs. 52–6; M. Rostovtzeff, *Social and Econ. History*, p. 76, pl. XII (with text). *Photographs after Mon. Piot*, v]

[*c*] ALTAR of MANLIUS (back). Restorations: none. A goddess, identified by the traces of a cornucopiae and the cup in her hand as a *Fortuna* or City-goddess (in this case of Caere, where the altar was found) sits enthroned in a high-backed chair, placed on a rocky base. On her right are three female figures heavily draped, with their hands raised in prayer; on her left three male figures. On the front face (not illustrated) a sacrifice in honour of the *Genius Augusti* (?) is offered by one C. Manlius. At the sides of the altar are represented statues of Lares on rocky brackets. The whole style, the tridimensional rendering and the attempt at foreshortening indicate a Claudian period verging to Neronian. In *Rome, Lateran.* (x, 480, 552.)

[*C.I.L.* x, 3616; Dessau, 6577; Helbig-Amelung, no. 1177; E. Strong, *op. cit.* I, figs. 36–37; O. Brendel, *op. cit.* p. 204. *Photograph Alinari*]

[c]

[a]

[b]

RELIEFS

ALTAR of the AUGUSTAN LARES. Restored: large pieces of the plinth. The altar is much battered; the top broken off and the edges damaged, but the central reliefs retain their original freshness of surface. Dedicated to Augustus by the S.P.Q.R. between 12 and 7 B.C. On the back [*a*]: Apotheosis of Caesar whose chariot rises heavenward; above on the left *Sol* in his chariot and on the right *Caelus* emerging to the waist from a cloud and holding out the cosmic mantle like a sail about his head. Traces of the eagle above *Sol*. On one side [*b*] of the altar is represented the consecration of the Lares: on the right Augustus *capite velato* offers the statuette of a Lar to a priest, also with veiled head, who holds another Lar in his right hand; each personage is accompanied by a couple of attendants; between the two is an altar decorated with garland and *patera* and laden with fruit; a festal garland also hangs between the pillars and above are *patera*, *urceus* and augural *lituus*. On the opposite side [*c*] Aeneas leaning on his staff contemplates the miracle of the sow in the presence of *Acca Larentia*, mother of the Lares, who sits on a rock reading out of the prophetic scroll. On the front face (not illustrated) is a Victory carrying a large shield with the inscription which names Augustus as Pontifex Maximus; the altar therefore cannot be earlier than 12 B.C. nor, as Gagé points out (*op. cit.* p. 76), is it likely to be much later than 7 B.C. when the cult of the Lares was finally re-established. (x, 480, 550.) In *Rome, Vatican*.

[*C.I.L.* VI, 876; W. Amelung, *Sc. des Vat.* II, pp. 242 *sqq.*; E. Strong, *Apotheosis*, pp. 66 *sqq.*; J. Gagé, *Mélanges*, XLIX, 1932, pp. 61 *sqq.*; L. R. Taylor, *The Divinity of the Roman Emperor*, p. 186. *Photographs German Institute*]

[a]

[b]

[c]

ALTAR of the VICOMAGISTRI. [a] On the front panel sacrifice of a bull and a boar is offered by the four *vicomagistri*, who, standing in pairs on each side of an altar, clasp hands across it. Around are grouped the attendants. On the left panel [b] a Lar in the usual dress stands on a small plinth. A similar figure (not illustrated) on the opposite side. At the back, much mutilated, traces of a large wreath. (x, 480, 551.) In *Rome, Palazzo d. Conservatori.*

[*C.I.L.* vi, 30957; B.S.R. *Cat. Pal. Cons.* p. 74, no. 2 (with reference to older literature); L. R. Taylor, *The Divinity of the Roman Emperor*, p. 186. *Photographs Faraglia*]

ALTAR of the GENS AUGUSTA. Restorations: none. The altar apparently belonged to a temple of which the inscription was found near by and which reads: *genti Augustae P. Perelius Hedulus sac. perp. templum solo privato primus pecunia propria fecit.* The date of the temple is uncertain. According to Gastinell it may have been erected as early as 27–15 B.C. On the other hand Rostovtzeff dates the altar as late as Tiberius and suggests that the original from which it was copied belonged possibly to the temple of Augustus on the Palatine erected by Tiberius. (For his later opinion see *Bull. des Antiquaires de France*, 1925, p. 209.) On the front face [*a*] Roma, wearing an Attic helmet and leaning on her shield, is seated on a pile of armour; her thin, loosely draped chiton and mantle, the dress of peace, shows that she has done with war. In her right hand the goddess holds a Victory and in front of her is placed obliquely an altar upon which rests the globe, symbol of world empire, with the cornucopiae, symbol of the fertility under Rome's rule, and the *caduceus*, herald of peace and plenty. For these symbols see also 124 [*b*]. This Roma type, which may be borrowed from that on the Ara Pacis, reappears on the base of Antoninus Pius (*Scult. Romana.* p. 246, fig. 151), all probably deriving from a now-lost canonical model going back to an Athena type (cf. coin of Lysimachus, *Volume of Plates* ii, 8 [*l*]). The panel unites in itself two ideas already familiar from the Ara Pacis: the imperial rule and the prosperity that it brings to the world. On the opposite face [*b*] sits Apollo, protector of the new *ordo Romanus*, with the griffin and his cithara on his left. He wears a laurel wreath and holds a laurel branch in his right hand. For the seated attitude Poinssot compares the Nolan relief with the Actian Apollo (see x, 553 and *Scult. Romana*, I, fig. 7) and the seated Augustus on the two cameos of Vienna (cf. 156 [*b*] below, and F. Eichler and E. Kris, *Die Kameen im Kunst Museum* (Vienna), no. 6, pl. 3). In front of the god is a tall tripod. For the notion that this Apollo repeats a type that existed on the Ara Pacis see Rostovtzeff, *op. cit.*, but this would demand the exclusion of the Terra Mater slab which in the present state of our knowledge seems untenable (see above, 120). On the third side: Aeneas on his flight from Troy carrying the aged Anchises on his left arm and leading Ascanius by the hand. The fourth side (not illustrated) shows, in a rather rough provincial style, a sacrifice generally interpreted as being offered by Augustus in honour of the patron gods of the gens Julia. The crowning of the altar is composed of two snakes. Imperial eagles adorn the acroteria. (x, 487, 552). Found in *Carthage*. Now in *Tunis, Musée du Bardo*.

[H. A. Merlin, *Bull. archéol.* CLXXXVI, 1919; M. Rostovtzeff, *Röm. Mitt.* XXXIX, 1923–4, p. 290 *sq.*, pls. 2–4; *Social and Econ. History*, p. 44, pl. VI; L. Poinssot, *L'autel de la Gens Augusta* (Notes et documents), 1929, p. 559; J. Sieveking, *Gnomon*, VII, 1931, p. 21; W. Tarn, *J.R.S.* XXII, 1932, p. 157. *Photographs after Poinssot, loc. cit.*]

[a]

[b]

RELIEFS

[a] FRIEZE with sacrifice of SUOVETAURILIA. Broken vertically towards the centre but correctly put together. The plinth with the feet and legs of nearly all the men and animals are restored; the left edge missing. A tall figure, presumably an emperor, is dropping incense at the first of twin altars. Behind these two trees. In the background, on the left of the officiant, a camillus holds an incense box and a second comes up with a jug. The procession falls into two groups; the first of attendants bringing up the boar and the ram; the second of those leading the bull; the two being united by a stately personage. Nearly all wear the festal wreath. In the background lictors, etc. The composition by masses, the freedom of the movements and disappearance of all stiffness show the relief, once regarded as Augustan, to be later. The date might be Tiberian and the tall figure Tiberius known for his stature (Suet. *Tib.* 58). R. West suggests the Emperor Gaius, who was likewise tall (Suet. *Cal.* 50). The face is too much damaged for identification. A later date, Claudio-Neronian verging to Flavian, is also possible. In *Paris, Louvre*. In the fifteenth century at Rome in Palazzo Venezia; then at Venice.

[E. Strong, *Scultura Romana*, I, p. 126; O. Brendel, *Röm. Mitt.* XLV, 1930, p. 202 (in favour of a Claudian date). *Photograph Louvre*]

[b] RELIEF from the BASE of PUTEOLI. Restorations: none. Erected according to the inscription on the front in A.D. 30 by the Augustales at Puteoli to commemorate the Emperor's bounty after the earthquakes that devastated Asia Minor in A.D. 17 and perhaps 18 (Tac. *Ann.* II, 47). The figures are probably adapted from the monument in Rome which consisted of a colossal Tiberius surrounded by statues (?) of the grateful cities set up in the Forum of Caesar near the temple of Venus (Platner-Ashby, p. 226). This relief from the back of the base comprises six figures: (1) *Temnos*, male figure cloaked and wearing high boots; (2) *Cibyra*, as an Amazon; (3) *Myrina*, with the tripod at her side in allusion to Apollo's neighbouring oracle. Behind the tripod a column supporting a statuette of Artemis is the attribute of (4) who, with left foot on the mask of a bearded river-god, personifies *Ephesus*. From her mural crown rise flames (?) alluding to the catastrophe, or perhaps antlers, symbols of the Ephesian Artemis; in her raised hand she holds corn and poppies. (5) *Apollonidea* (sic = *Apollonis Lydiae*), in the background, wears a turreted crown and holds an animal (?); (6) possibly *Hyrcanis*, distinguishing attributes and inscription effaced. Cf. the sixty Gallic cities that stood round the altar of the *Tres Galliae* at Lugdunum (Strabo IV, 192). Found at Pozzuoli in 1793; cf. two fragments from Smyrna in the Louvre, from a similar monument (Reinach, *R.R.* II, 299, 2, 3). In *Naples, Museo Nazionale*. (x, 554.)

[*C.I.L.* X, 1624; *Guida Ruesch*, no. 82; Brunn-Bruckmann (Sieveking), pl. 575; E. Strong, *op. cit.* p. 93, pl. XVIII; O. Brendel, *loc. cit. Photograph Alinari*]

[a]

[b]

[a] GILT BRONZE PLAQUE, from sword-sheath. In the centre Tiberius sits enthroned, his drapery loosely flung across his lower limbs (cf. the Tiberius on the Grand Camée 156 [b] and the statues 152 [b] and [c]). His identity is made certain by the shield inscribed *Felicitas Tiberii* on the ground on his left. With his right hand he receives a Victory brought to him by Germanicus, who stands facing him. Between the two is *Mars Ultor* armed and holding a shield and spear. Behind the imperial group advances a figure of Victory holding a shield inscribed *Victoria Augusti*. The scene is the return of Germanicus in A.D. 16 after his operations beyond the Rhine. His successes were won by the prowess of the young general but in happy collaboration with the mystical forces represented by the imperial *Felicitas* or Luck and by the *Victoria* inherent in the house of Augustus. The same idea was conveyed by the inscription on the arch erected in the Roman Forum in A.D. 16 in honour of both Germanicus and Tiberius, where the inscription recorded by Tacitus reads: *fine anni arcus propter aedem Saturni ob recepta signa cum Varro amissa ductu Germanici auspiciis Tiberii et . . . dicantur* (Tac. *Ann.* II, 41). The scene recalls the central part of the Grand Camée (156 [b]); but on the Camée the group is invested with a transcendental character in contrast with the more actual rendering on the sword-sheath. The other details of the sheath (not illustrated) are likewise interesting: in the centre a head of Tiberius laureate and, at the point, a temple within which there appear a Roman eagle and standards; immediately below an amazon-clad figure is sometimes explained as representing the conquered region. The sword inside the sheath was of iron. Found near Mainz in 1848; since 1866 in the *British Museum*. (x, 554.)

[*C.I.L.* XIII, 6797; J. Gagé, *Rev. Arch.* XXXII, 1930, pp. 1 *sqq.*; *Brit. Mus. Bronzes*, no. 867. *Photograph British Museum*]

[b, c] Two bronze beam ends with HEADS of WOLVES. The heads were found in 1929 in the recent operations for recovering the ships of Nemi; they are similar in style to the two found in 1895, now in the Museo delle Terme (Paribeni, no. 1142, ed. 1929). These heads decorated the square bronze castings at the ends of the wooden beams with evident apotropaic intention. (x, 555.) In the little museum on the *Lake of Nemi*.

[G. Cultrera, *Not. Sc.* 1932, p. 284. *Photographs lent by Dr Cultrera*]

[a]

[b]

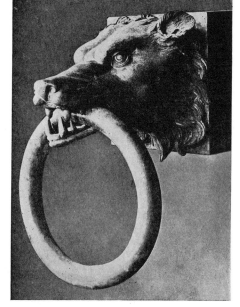

[c]

BRONZE AND SILVER

[a] BRONZE HEAD of MEDUSA from one of the Nemi ships. The head adorned the casing of a beam end (cf. 140 [b, c]). Compared with the Lauersfort Medusa (142 [b]) the forms appear coarser and the large staring eyes have a less concentrated expression; the eyebrows are decorative but without distinction; the flying locks of hair are asymmetric; altogether a more brutal version of the Medusa type. At the same time in comparing the Nemi and the Lauersfort Medusa we must remember that the former was intended to adorn a boat and was only seen at a distance, the forms therefore, in order to be telling, must be somewhat violent, whereas the more classic forms of the Lauersfort Medusa may be due to the fact that the ornament was to be seen at close range. The informing spirit is the same. These Gorgons, whether or not composed as medallions, may be compared to the apotropaic or protective medallion heads on each side of the arch of Augustus at Rimini (192 [a]) or to the Juppiter Ammon medallions of the Forum Augusti or again to the so-called Medusa of Bath. In *Rome, Museo delle Terme.* (x, 556.)

[Helbig-Amelung, 1522; *Not. Scav.* 1895, p. 372. *Photograph Alinari*]

[b] MEDUSA HEAD on a PHALERA. One of ten similar pieces (diam. 10–11 cm.) which adorned the breast-plate of one Gaius Flavius Festus. The incised eyebrows are connected by frowning lines that almost form a triangle; the pupils are sunk; nose and lips are severely modelled; the lips though full are tightly compressed with projection of the under lip. The locks lie symmetrically against the skull. Above the head two tiny snakes form a ring round the locks that part to either side to frame the face in a wave pattern. The work is dated by Matz to the transition phase that follows upon Augustan art; Pernice, *op. cit.* p. 87, inclines to date it as late as the Flavian period. Classical influence is evident; cf. the Medusa of the Ptolemy vase and the Medusas of the Campana reliefs. In *Berlin*; found at *Lauersfort*, in the district of Moers on the Lower Rhine, in 1858.

[F. Matz, Berlin. *Winckelm. Programm*, XCII, 1932; E. Pernice, *Die Hellenistische Kunst in Pompeii*, Part V, 1932, pp. 36 *sqq.*]

[c] BUST of PSYCHE on a PHALERA. Psyche is looking over her shoulder as though towards the Cupid of another Medallion (see x, 556). Her wreath of ivy berries is held together by a twisted ribbon. Other bunches of ivy berries are above the ears. The child, breathless with running, sinks her head between her shoulders as if in terror of her pursuer. The forms of nose, mouth and chin recall the Cupid (118 [d]). The same Cupid and Psyche theme occurs on two panels of a Hellenistic bronze chest at Pompeii (Pernice, *op. cit.* Pls. 53, 54). The medallions are of gilt silver and are attached to a copper backing inscribed in most instances MEDAMI, whether the name of the artist or of a workshop is uncertain. For the arrangement of such phalerae on a breast-plate cf. the tombstone of the centurion Caelius in the Museum of Bonn. In *Berlin*; found at *Lauersfort*.

[*Photographs lent by Dr Matz*]

[a]

[b]

[c]

RELIEFS

[*a*] BRONZE GLADIATORIAL HELMET with Trojan scenes. One of two bronze helmets with traces of gilding, found at *Pompeii* in the barracks of the gladiators and richly ornamented with figures and groups in relief. On the 'cap' against the battlemented walls of Troy, which are only slightly indicated, are the following groups in high relief: Ajax and Cassandra; Neoptolemus slaying Priam; Menelaus and Helen; Aeneas carrying Anchises; Aeneas, Creusa (?) and Ascanius. On the cheekpieces in lower relief, right, Sinon led away by two Trojans; left, Sinon before Priam. Crest and brim similarly decorated with scenes (religious?) as yet imperfectly made out. The episodes of the 'cap' are evidently excerpts from more extensive picture illustrations of the Trojan War such as came into fashion in Hellenistic times; scenes from the Iliupersis were specially popular in the Augustan period with its awakened interest in the Trojan ancestry of Rome. The helmet however would seem to be of a later date than Augustus, perhaps Tiberian, Tiberius having specially encouraged pictorial chronicles relating to Troy (cf. *B.S.R. Cat. of Mus. Capitol*, p. 170). In *Naples*. (x, 556.)

[Reinach, *R.R.* iii, p. 76, 2–3; p. 77, 1; A. Mau, *Pompei*, ed. 1907, pp. 163 *sqq.*; *Guida Ruesch*, no. 1897; H. Heydemann, *Iliupersis*, pp. 32 *sqq.*; Niccolini, *Case e pitture di Pompei*, Caserma dei gladiatori, ii, 8; iii, 11–21. *Photograph Alinari*]

[*b*] RELIEF with emblems of Jupiter. Restorations: none; the back of the eagle, the tip of its wings and other projecting parts of the relief were broken but are antique and correctly mended. The composition is perfectly self-contained within its frame. The relief must be held entirely distinct from the reliefs of Cupids carrying attributes of the gods, now scattered in different places (the two best known being walled in at S. Vitale in Ravenna), which formed part of a frieze from a monument destroyed in the middle ages; their somewhat frigid style is generally referred to as 'neo-attic.' The more animated style of the Mantua piece, the superb fling of the drapery, the proud mien of the eagle seem to indicate a later, perhaps Claudian, period. On the right side is seen the throne of the god and a small Cupid (wing and lower part only preserved) helping to support the huge thunderbolt (for other details see x, 556). The attributes of Juppiter are probably used here as imperial emblems recalling the frequent identification of the Roman Emperor with *Juppiter Capitolinus*; see Augustus as Jupiter on the Gemma Augustea (below 156 [*a*]), the Blacas cameo, etc.; also Tiberius as Juppiter (152 [*c*] and [*d*]; 156 [*b*]), and elsewhere. In *Mantua*, Palazzo Ducale.

[A. Levi, *Sculture del Pal. Ducale*, pl. 84; *id.* Historia, iii, 1929, pp. 270 *sqq.* *Photograph supplied by Drssa A. Levi*]

[a]

[b]

[a] AUGUSTUS from *Prima Porta*, in the *Vatican*. Restored: parts of left ear and left shoulder; four fingers of the right hand; left index; the sceptre and parts of the back and mantle. Left leg and right arm have been broken. Traces of colour: brown for hair; iris of eyes outlined in red; fringe of shoulder-flaps rose-pink; upper part of breast-plate likewise pink (an unusual colour for a breast-plate); all the symbolic figures once picked out in a variety of colours. (For details see Amelung, *op. cit.*) The statue—a master-piece of Roman portraiture—is generally held, from the central scene on the breast-plate, to commemorate the Parthian events of 20 B.C. and is therefore dated to 19 B.C. or soon after. But the advanced style of the head as well as the details of the breast-plate (a vision of empire impossible to art in so complete a form as early in the Principate as 19 B.C.) suggests a later date. It might even be attributed to the time of Claudius, whose desire to glorify Augustus is well known. That the statue was found in the villa of Livia at Prima Porta says nothing against a later date since the villa con-tinued to be imperial property long after the death of Augustus. The portrait, however, is evidently based on a contemporary like-ness. The Emperor wears a short chiton beneath his cuirass; from which depend long leather tabs each adorned with twisted fringes; similar tabs appear at the armholes (see 150). The large military cloak is slung round the hips, both ends hanging down over the left forearm. For details of the cuirass see 150 (x, 6, 263, 557*sq.*). The small Cupid (see 118 [*d*]) on a dolphin alludes to the divine descent of Augustus, the dolphin possibly being likewise a symbol of fertility.

[W. Amelung, *Skulpturen d. Vatican*, I, p. 19, no. 14; Helbig-Amelung, no. 5; E. Loewy, *Röm. Mitt.* XLII, 1927, pp. 200 *sqq. Photograph Arti grafiche, Bergamo*]

[b] AUGUSTUS from *Via Labicana*, in the *Museo delle Terme, Rome*. Restorations: none. The head is in a different marble to the body. The Emperor wears a short-sleeved chiton beneath the toga, which is richly draped and drawn over the back of the head as usual in sacrificing. That the Emperor is here represented as officiating at an altar, probably as Pontifex Maximus, is sufficiently borne out by the movement of what remains of the right arm. The left hand, now missing, probably held a *rotulus*. The feet are lightly clad in the *calceus*. Found in 1910 in Via Labicana within the city. (x, 6, 558.)

[*Notizie degli Scavi*, 1910, p. 223 *sq.*; Paribeni, *Museo d. Terme*, no. 101; Helbig-Amelung, no. 1528; R. Paribeni, pl. 114; Curtius in *Röm. Mitt.* XLVII, 1932, p. 248. *Photograph Museo delle Terme*]

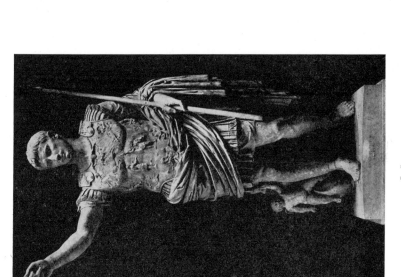

[*a*] THE YOUNG TIBERIUS; in *Boston*. The head is detached from
a statue in which Tiberius was represented offering sacrifice with
drapery drawn over the back of his head. The features are of the
greatest delicacy; the cranium is of remarkable breadth as in all
his accredited portraits. The beautifully shaped and well-opened
eyes agree with the testimony of the authors as to the eyes in later
life (evidence in Bernoulli). (x, 560.)

[L. D. Caskey, *Mus. Fine Arts Boston, Catal. Greek and Roman Sculpture*, 1925,
no. 111, p. 248 *sq. Photograph Museum of Fine Arts, Boston*]

[*b*] SEATED STATUE found at *Privernum* in 1795. In the *Vatican,
Museo Chiaramonti*. Restored: nose, parts of upper lip, of the chin
and of the right ear; both forearms, the left with part of the mantle;
left hand, right foot and part of the left; seat and plinth. The
attitude of the Emperor is similar to that of the following statue
and, like it, is borrowed from a seated Juppiter type. The drapery
leaves the back bare and the Emperor wears no wreath. From the
movement of arms and hands it is clear that the Emperor held a
sceptre with his left and probably a thunderbolt with his right,
insignia borrowed, like those of the *triumphator*, from Juppiter.
(x, 560.)

[W. Amelung, *Skulpturen d. Vatican*, I, Chiaramonti, no. 494; Helbig-Amelung,
no. 90; R. West, p. 173, pl. XLIII, fig. 183. *Photograph Anderson*]

[*c*] COLOSSAL SEATED STATUE found at *Caere*, in the *Lateran
Museum, Rome*. Restored: nose; ends of the *taenia*. The Emperor
wearing the oak crown (*corona civica*) sits enthroned like Juppiter,
the mantle flung over his legs and covering his back but leaving
bare his breast. His right shoulder is sunk, the left raised. The right
hand possibly held the thunderbolt, the left the sceptre—both
attributes of the god from whom the attitude is borrowed. The
Emperor is shown young as in the Louvre statue and that from
Veii in the Vatican. (x, 560.)

[Helbig-Amelung, no. 1167; R. West, p. 172. For portraits of Tiberius see also R.
Hinks, *J.R.S.* XXIII, 1933, p. 34 (from Majorca); G. Oliverio, *Africa Italiana*, III,
1930, p. 201, fig. 58 (from Benghazi); L. Ugolini, *Bull. del. Museo dell' Impero Romano*,
1931, pp. 21 *sqq.* (from Malta). *Photograph Alinari*]

[a]

[b]

[c]

[a] GEMMA AUGUSTEA, in *Vienna*. Sardonyx, lower, darker layer for background, white for figures. In centre Roma, helmeted, and Augustus; sceptre, and eagle under the throne, equate him with Juppiter; he holds augural staff; his left foot on a shield (*clipeus aureus* in the curia Julia?). A figure (? the *Oikumene*) holds a *corona civica* (cf. *Res Gestae* 34). Above a capricorn, his natal constellation. Beside 'Oikumene' are *Oceanus* (?) and *Terra Mater* with cornucopiae, and two children. On the left (a piece missing here) the warrior descending from his chariot may be Tiberius in the triumph of A.D. 12 (Suetonius, *Tib*. 20); the young man by the horses may be Germanicus. Alternatively this is the triumph of the German campaign of 7 B.C., in which Gaius Caesar took part, being at that time 13 (about the age of the boy on the cameo), Tiberius being 35. In the exergue Roman soldiers erect a trophy and on the right are captives. (x, 568, 609.) In the opinion of the present writer the originals of these cameos were triumphal pictures or reliefs (see *Apotheosis and After-life*, p. 67 *sq.*; Gagé, *op. cit.* p. 28 *sq.*) set up soon after the events commemorated. The cameos may have been presents to foreign potentates, which would account for the supposed finding of this and the *Grand Camée* (below) in the East.

[b] *The Grand Camée de France*, in the *Cabinet de Médailles, Paris*. Sardonyx in five layers. A synopsis of interpretations in Bernoulli (*op. cit.* p. 278 *sq.*), whose own is still the most satisfactory. In the centre Tiberius as Juppiter and Livia as Ceres (?); he has aegis, sceptre, and *lituus* held out to a young warrior who may be Germanicus (cf. the Mainz sheath, 140 [a]) receiving the auspices for the coming campaign. Between them Antonia (?), mother of Germanicus. The boy is the Emperor Gaius (born A.D. 12) as the darling of the army, in military dress, his feet on piled armour. Beside the boy his mother Agrippina. Behind the throne is perhaps the Younger Drusus, with his wife Drusilla (sister of Germanicus), pointing upwards to a figure, riding the winged horse of apotheosis, certainly Germanicus (died A.D. 19 in the East). A winged boy leads the horse towards Augustus, who reclines supported by a Phrygian-clad figure (? Aeneas or Ascanius-Iulus). A warrior advancing from the left should be Nero Drusus, father of Germanicus; the seated Oriental by the throne may be an Arsacid hostage. In the exergue, Germanic prisoners and a Parthian; flanking these a river god and armour.

A new theory of L. Curtius, who believes the cameo to refer to Gaius wearing the armour of Alexander and that the Persian-clad figure is Alexander himself, will be published in *Röm. Mitt.* 1934 (x, 568, 634.)

[Eichler-Kris, *Die Kameen im Kunsth. Mus.* no. 7, pl. 4; F. West, p. 137, pl. XXXIV, 148; J. Bernoulli, *Römische Ikonographie*, II, pp. 262 *sqq.*, 275 *sqq.*; J. Gagé, *Rev. Arch.* XXXII, 1930, pp. 19 *sqq.*, 29 *sqq.*; H. Schrader, 'Ikonographie der Himmelfahrt' in *Warburg Vorträge*, VIII (1928), pp. 99 *sqq*. *Photographs after* A. Furtwängler, *Antike Gemmen*, pls. LVI, LX]

[a]

[b]

RELIEF AND BRONZE

[a] RELIEF with members of the Julio-Claudian family, in *Ravenna*. Restorations: none. The edges are not clean cut as in the photograph but jagged, as the piece was continued both to right and left. The fragments as now put together in the Ravenna Museum come too close to the personages of the centre. Identifications of the personages are almost as numerous as of those on the Grand Camée. The question is complicated by the loss of the right half of the slab. On the extreme right is Augustus with oak-wreath, sceptre or spear (now lost), mantle, left foot on world-globe, represented taller than the personages on his right and looking away from them. The attitude, as pointed out first by Bernoulli (*loc. cit.*), is that of the bronze Augustus-Juppiter of Naples. The diademed figure at his side, with a Cupid on her left shoulder (traces only preserved), must be Livia as *Venus Genetrix* (cf. Boscoreale cups, 128 [a], [b]). Next comes a young man who held out an object (now lost) to a tall military figure. No satisfactory interpretation has been proposed for the first; the soldier undoubtedly resembles Agrippa (see Poulsen, *loc. cit.*; cf. 154 [a]). According to Poulsen the two represent Marcellus, already deified, handing the *parazonium* to his successor, Agrippa. The female figure seated on a rock (partially destroyed) on the left is probably *Roma*, or *Terra Mater*, balancing some similar conception on the opposite side. The relief curves curiously outward at the top, so that it can hardly have decorated either a temple or an arch. Evidently the personages portrayed are conceived as presiding at a sacrifice. From the left advances the bull, girt with ornamental sash and led by the sacrificial attendants (cf. the *suovetaurilia* relief in the Louvre, 138 [a]). Their movements are less stiff than those on the Louvre relief, though on both the two figures immediately behind the bull turn to one another with identical attitude. (x, 561.)

[J. Bernoulli, *op. cit.* II, pp. 254 *sqq.*; E. Strong, *Scultura Romana*, p. 95; F. Poulsen, *Porträtstatuen in norditalienischen Provinzmuseen*, pp. 61 *sqq. Photograph Alinari*]

[b] BRONZE HORSE from a quadriga; *St Mark's, Venice*. The group of bronze gilt horses came to Venice from Constantinople in the beginning of the thirteenth century. That the group is much older than the erection of Constantinople into a capital is evident from the style. They were possibly brought to the new Rome from the old. By comparison with horses from Pompeii and Herculaneum (e.g. the equestrian statues of the Balbi at Naples), which can be dated to the time of Augustus, it is clear that they fall into the same series and should be dated to the early Empire. (x, 563.)

[Kluge-Lehmann-Hartleben, II, p. 78 *sq.*, fig. 7, with older bibliography. *Photograph Anderson*]

[a]

[b]

[*a*] BRONZE BUST, in *New York*. Restorations: none. Preservation almost perfect. The intense expression is largely due to the ivory eye-balls (antique). In the development of Roman portraiture it belongs to the period in which the harsher and earlier treatment yields to the more harmonious manner of Augustan art. (x, 562.)

[G. Richter, *Metr. Mus. Bronzes*, no. 325; Kluge-Lehmann-Hartleben, II, p. 11, fig. 4. *Photograph Metropolitan Museum, New York*]

[*b*] BRONZE portrait of NORBANUS SOREX, in *Naples*. The eyes are now missing. Winckelmann still saw them and says that the whites were of marble. The head is inserted into a herm inscribed: *C. Norbanus Sorex secundarum mag. pagi Aug. Felicis suburbanum ex d.d.loc.d.* From this inscription the head has been dated to the period of Sulla, Sorex being identified with the actor Sorix named by Plutarch as a protégé of Sulla (Plutarch, *Sulla*, 36). But through the Norbanus Sorex of the herm was an actor *secundarum partium* it is difficult to maintain the Sullan date, not only for reasons of style but also because a *pagus Augusti* could not have existed before 27 B.C. when Octavian became *Augustus*, or indeed before 7 B.C. when Augustus restored the cult of the Lares with which the *magistri pagi* are connected. The facial forms and the treatment suggest a Tiberian date (x, 562); Goethert favours a Flavian date, while Brendel detects Egyptian influence. Found at *Pompeii* in the temple of Isis.

[*C.I.L.* x, 814; Ruesch, no. 929; Arndt-Bruckmann, pl. 457; Kluge-Lehmann-Hartleben, II, p. 4, fig. 1; F. W. Goethert, p. 23; O. Brendel, *Antike*, 1933, p. 138 *sq.*; M. Bieber, *Denkmäler zum Theaterwesen im Altertum*, 1930, p. 177, no. 190. *Photograph Alinari*]

[*c, d*] JULIO-CLAUDIAN PORTRAIT, in *Rome, Capitoline Museum*. Restored: edges of ears; otherwise the preservation is excellent. The workmanship, which is of the first order, is obviously Claudian; for a characterization of the personage see x, 562.

[*B.S.R. Cat. of Cap. Mus.* Colombe, no. 64; L. Curtius, *Antike*, VII, 1931, p. 231, pl. 23. *Photographs German Institute*]

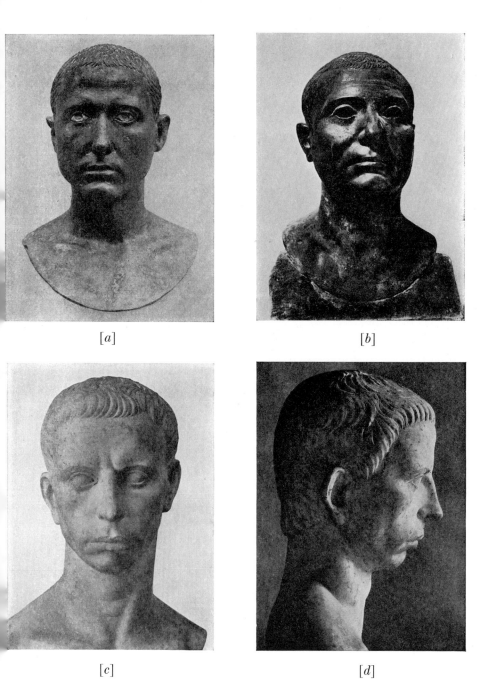

[a]

[b]

[c]

[d]

BUST of a GIRL, in *Rome, Museo Torlonia*, found at *Vulci*. Restorations: none. Missing: parts of the hairdressing, of the ears and the eyeballs which were inset. The shape of the bust, which is unusual for Roman portraits, assimilates to that of the Greco-Roman herm. The girl wears a delicately worked chiton gathered into a band. The fashion of the hair is a little older than the time of the Second Triumvirate (see 166 [*d*]). Details (the chignon and parts of the temples) must have been added in stucco or bronze as the holes round the head indicate. For a description and characterization of the head see x, 563.

[G. Kaschnitz-Weinberg, p. 204; *Bemerkungen*, p. 184; R. Bianchi Bandinelli, p. 85. *Photographs German Institute*]

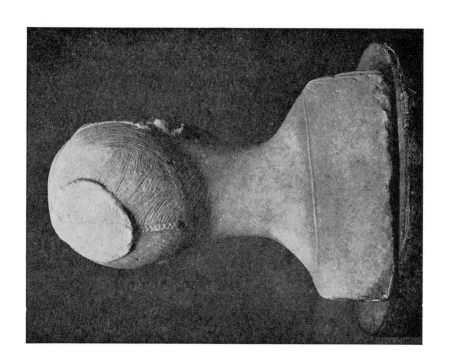

[a] Head of OCTAVIA of green basalt, in the *Louvre*. Provenance unknown but, from the unusual material and from the fact that the replica in Bonn was found in Egypt, perhaps Egypt. Restorations: none. The clear-cut features rendered by a masterly technique bear witness to the beauty of Octavian's sister, to whom he erected statues on her return from Greece after she had been deserted by Antony (Dio 49, 38). The characteristic hairdressing can be dated to the years 43–35 by coins of Antony (cf. 56 [k]). (x, 51, 564.)

[*Cat. somm. Louvre*, no. 1233; F. Winter, *Bonner Jahrb.* 1925, p. 69; F. W. Goethert, p. 34; R. West, p. 106, pl. XXVI, 104; R. Paribeni, pl. 121. *Photograph Alinari*]

[b] Head of LIVIA, found in *Rome*; in *Copenhagen, Glyptotek Ny Carlsberg*. Restored: lower part of the nose. Traces of brown colour on pupils and hair, excellent preservation. The head, which is admirably carved, is that of an energetic and clever woman. The features show a striking resemblance to her sons Tiberius (see x, 564) and Nero Drusus. For the novel hairdressing in waves and fringed ringlets see x, 546. The signs of age—sunk eyes and sagging cheeks—are forgotten in the nobility of the mien and the imperial glance.

[Arndt-Bruckmann, pls. 6–7; Delbrueck, *op. cit.* pl. 34 (with bibl.); R. West, p. 128, pl. XXX, 130; R. Paribeni, pl. 115. *Photograph Ny Carlsberg Glyptotek*]

[c] Head of the ELDER AGRIPPINA, found in the sanctuary of Apollo at *Cyrene*. The head was inserted into a statue. There are existing two types of Agrippina portraits, possibly referring to the two periods in which the erecting of statues for her is known: in the years A.D. 17–19, after the triumph of her husband Germanicus, and after her death in A.D. 33, but not till her son Gaius became Emperor. Anti suggests the Cyrene portrait belongs to the former group as representing an individual personage full of character and life, though it appears older in age than the second group known from the head in the Capitol (*B.S.R. Cat. Imperatori*, no. 10, etc.), which, however, must be the more idealized representation of the dead Agrippina and therefore with younger but more generalized features. Excellent work and preservation. (x, 546.)

[C. Anti, *Africa Italiana*, 1928, pp. 3 *sqq.*; R. Paribeni, pl. 136. *Photograph from Prof. Anti*]

[d] BRONZE head of a GIRL, in *Parma, Palazzo Farnese*. Found at *Velleja* in 1760. Restorations: none. In style somewhat later than the head of Museo Torlonia (164); the date may be early Augustan. The holes on the raised surface of the hair, the purpose of which is uncertain, probably served for the attachment of looser locks. The parting is covered by a narrow plait. For a fuller description see x, 564.

[Arndt-Bruckmann, pls. 89, 90; Kluge-Lehmann-Hartleben, II, p. 6, fig. 4; Kaschnitz-Weinberg, p. 206; *Bemerkungen*, p. 185; R. Bianchi Bandinelli, p. 89; R. West, p. 100, pl. XXV, 97. *Photograph German Institute*]

[a]

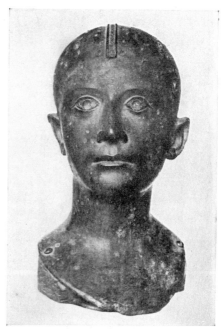

[d]

[b]

[c]

PORTRAIT

Head and shoulders of a statue of LIVIA, in *Pompeii, Villa dei Misteri*. Missing: edge of the mantle over the head and the diadem which must have been in the hair. *Colours* preserved but much faded from exposure to the air: pupils of eyes *brown*; iris *black*; hair and eyebrows *reddish*; mouth *red*; edges of mantle and tunic *purple*. The head, which appears too smal lfor the body, could not belong originally to the statue though already adjusted to it in Roman times. The head is admirably worked and perfectly preserved. The identification as Livia is arrived at by comparison with the rest of her portraiture. At first sight it seems difficult to account for the statue being found in a private villa which was neither an imperial domain nor specially connected with the Empress. Maiuri accordingly conjectures that the statue was placed here in a private house in connection with the cult of the Lares (cf. the portrait of Livia found in a *Lararium* of a villa in Gragnano, near Naples, and another in a Gallo-Roman villa near *Lugdunum*). The style of the head seems later than Augustan, according to Maiuri Tiberian or even Claudian. (x, 561.)

[A. Maiuri, *Villa dei Misteri*, pp. 223 *sqq. Photographs supplied by Professor Maiuri*]

PAINTING AND MOSAIC

[*a*] WALL-PAINTING from the Villa of Livia at *Prima Porta* (detail); in *Rome*. The painting, which covers the four walls of a sunk or garden room, is intended to afford to the spectator within the room itself a glimpse into a rich shrubbery of trees, fruit-trees and flowering plants, with birds flitting among the branches. The shrubbery is railed off from a strip of flower beds by a marble (?) baluster and the garden strip again is separated from the actual room by a low trellis. The painting is of the middle of the first century B.C., of about the same date as the paintings of the House of Livia on the Palatine. The Villa can be confidently identified with the Villa *ad Gallinas*, mentioned by Suetonius (*Galba*, I), and by Pliny (who gives the exact distance from Rome *iuxta nonum lapidem Flaminia Via, N.H.* xv, 137; cf. Dio Cassius XLVIII, 52), while the name continued in use to the Middle Ages. The property was probably inherited by Livia from her father, who died in 42 B.C. (she married Octavian in 38 B.C.), and the rooms with the paintings, being the oldest of the building, presumably date from about this epoch. In confirmation of this date it should be noted that the reticulate of the Villa and the House of Livia on the Palatine are of similar character. It is sometimes supposed that the comparatively good preservation of the paintings is due to the fact that this lower part was blocked during early Imperial renovations, these rooms remaining buried until excavated in 1863. Of recent years the paintings have lamentably faded. (x, 566.)

[Rizzo, p. 79 and pls. 180–182; Swindler, p. 341 and fig. 547. For the full publication see *Antike Denkmäler*, I, pl. 11 (and p. 4), pl. 24 (and p. 11), pl. 60 (and p. 52). The west hall has been described botanically by H. Möller, *Röm. Mitt.* 1890, pp. 78 *sqq.* See also H. Sulze in *Röm. Mitt.* XLVII, 1932, pp. 176 *sqq.* For a history of the building down to the time of Theodoric see G. Lugli in *Bull. Com.* 1923, pp. 26 *sqq.* *Photograph German Institute*]

[*b*] Fountain-niche decorated in MOSAIC. *Fitzwilliam Museum, Cambridge*. The niche is in the form of an apse with semi-dome decorated with a shell-pattern. The lower part is adorned, much in the style of the Prima Porta paintings, with a tangle of trees and flowering shrubs, while birds are seen flying in the open space above. The colour scheme of the foliage is in dull yellow ochre and sage green. A low baluster, upon which perches a peacock, fences off the shrubbery (cf. 172 [*a*]). Style and composition recall the pomegranate garden of the Casa dell' Efebo at Pompeii (Maiuri, *Pompeii*, p. 69, fig. 77) and the wall painting with trees and birds seen behind columns in the 'Villa del Menandro' (Maiuri, *Casa del Menandro*, pl. XI). (x, 567.) Cf. also the fountain niche at Pompeii, and the well-known example in the Lateran, with Silvanus, from the Mithraeum of Ostia (Helbig-Amelung, no. 1235).

[a]

[b]

[*a*] Portrait of VIRGIL in MOSAIC; from *Susa* in North Africa. In the *Musée de Bardo, Tunis*. White ground, within a border of red, white and black. The features homely, the body long and sinewy (Suetonius-Donatus 8). The poet sits on chair with high round back, his feet on a stool. His white toga, which shows a blue stripe, is closely folded about his body. The flesh parts are brown, the hair severely cut in Republican or early Augustan fashion (cf. 174 [*c*]). The attitude is stiff, the expression tense. The impression produced is of a copy (with the two Muses added) after a contemporary portrait. On his knees Virgil holds a papyrus roll open at the line: *Musa mihi causas memora, quo numine laeso.* (x, 570.)

[P. Gauchler in *Mon. Piot*, IV, 1897, pp. 233 *sqq.*; Swindler, p. 428 and fig. 639; B. Nogara, 'Ritratti di Virgilio' in *Rivista del R. Istituto di Archeol. e Storia d'Arte*, II, 1930, pp. 127 *sqq. Photograph Giraudon*]

[*b*] PORTRAIT of the poet MENANDER (lived 342–291 B.C.), in an exedra of the casa del Menandro at *Pompeii*. The poet is represented as young, in easy posture on a chair of ample proportions with curving back and legs and a red cushion. The heavy *himation* is white with greenish shadows; the flesh a reddish brown; in the thick hair are traces of an ivy wreath. The mantle is thrown over the left shoulder, but otherwise leaves the whole upper part of the body uncovered, in Greek fashion. The eyes are turned listlessly towards the open papyrus-roll inscribed *Menander*, followed by the words *hic primus* [novam?] *comediam scripsit . . . Libri quattuor* (see Maiuri, *op. cit.* p. 112 *sö.*). According to Technau (*op. cit.*) the painting may be after one in the Pompeion at Athens. (x, 570.)

[W. Technau, *Arch. Anzeiger*, 1932, p. 505. *Photograph after* A. Maiuri, *Casa del Menandro*, I, pp. 111 *sqq.*, plate XII and figs. 51, 52]

[*c*] Bust-length PORTRAIT-GROUP of a young man and his wife; from *Pompeii*, in *Naples*. The man, who has close-cropped hair, slight moustache and beard, and wears a white tunic and mantle, hold in his right hand a *rotulus* with its red label (probably the marriage contract as on marriage sarcophagi). Slightly in front of him stands his wife, with hair kept close to the head and bound by a ribbon but escaping in ringlets over the forehead. She wears a brown garment, her left hand holds a diptych and her right a stilus against her lips. The eyes are almond-shaped but well open; the ears are prominent as in Republican Roman portraiture. The two figures are imagined looking out from a square window-frame (only the lower ledge is visible in the illustration). The usual opinion derived from the ringlets worn by the woman is that the date is Claudian, but Curtius (*op. cit.* p. 379) proposes an earlier date, Augustan or Tiberian, because of the coiffures. The man has been called Paquius Proculus and, more recently, Terentius Neo (*studiosus iuris*). (x, 570.)

[Curtius, pl. XII; Rizzo, p. 83; P. Marconi, p. 53 and pl. 62; Della Corte in *J.R.S.* XVI, 1926, p. 151 *sq. Photograph Alinari*]

[a]

[b]

[c]

[a], [b] ROMULUS, and AENEAS. The paintings were found in 1913, on each side of the entrance to a house in the Via dell' Abbondanza in *Pompeii*. They have been recognized as imitations of the statues of Aeneas with Anchises and Ascanius, and of Romulus shouldering the spoils of Acron, which were among the effigies of illustrious Romans placed in the niches of the exedrae of the Forum of Augustus (x, 569, 578, 582). Cf. Ovid, *Fasti*, v, 563–6:

> Hinc videt Aenean oneratum pondere caro
> Et tot Iuleae nobilitatis avos;
> Hinc videt Iliaden umeris ducis arma ferentem
> Claraque dispositis acta subesse viris.

The description applies, word for word, to the Pompeian pictures. Copies, as we gather from the extant *elogia*, were made for the monuments of Eumachia at Pompeii and it is perhaps from these rather than from the prototype in Rome that our two pictures were taken. J. Gagé, who has worked up the whole question, has shown that copies likewise adorned the pediment of the Temple of the Divus Augustus in Rome. In [a] Romulus appears in Roman military dress with sword on his left hanging from his sword belt, and carrying his spear in his right hand; from his shoulders hangs a red cloak; he carries supported against his left arm the celebrated spoils (cf. Plutarch, *Romulus*, xvi, 16). In [b] Aeneas is represented carrying Anchises, who clasps the casket that holds the sacred Penates; Ascanius (Iulus), in red cloak and green Phrygian cap, runs along in front of his father who, however, grasps him by the hand. The cuirass of Aeneas is yellow (for gold) fringed with white (for silver) and is worn over a dark red tunic; cf. 204 [d].

[*Notizie degli Scavi*, 1913, p. 144 (Della Corte); M. Camaggio in *Accademia Pontaniana*, 1928, pp. 4 *sqq.*; J. Gagé in *Mélanges d'arch. et d'histoire*, 1930; Rizzo, pl. 107, p. 86.]

[c] The 'Origins of Rome,' from *Pompeii*, in *Naples*. The scene is laid on the Palatine; the narrative runs from the top of the picture to the bottom. Above, against the sky, appears the chariot of Diana and—dominating the whole composition—Mars, the divine ancestor, fully armed descending towards Rhea Sylvia, sleeping in a meadow. Shepherds, huts, shrines and a number of figures decorate the landscape. Below, Rhea appears once more guided by Hermes, who points out to her the twins in the cave nursed by the wolf. The picture is primarily a landscape, enlivened in the manner of the Odyssey landscapes by the introduction of a number of small figures taken, in this instance, from a Roman myth. It belongs to the class of pictures labelled as 'third Pompeian style.' (x, 569.)

[Hermann-Bruckmann, pl. 155 and p. 214; E. Rizzo, pl. 195; P. Marconi, *Pittura*, fig. 106 and p. 79; G. Marchietti-Longhi in *Capitolium*, ix, 1933, p. 377. *All three from original photographs kindly given by Prof. Maiuri*]

[a]

[b]

[c]

MOSAIC AND MARBLE

[*a*] MOSAIC: basket of flowers, in the *Vatican*; found in 1792 at *Roma Vecchia* in the Villa of the Quintilii, the brothers murdered by order of Commodus, *c.* A.D. 182; it has accordingly been attributed to the end of the second century, but the natural forms of the flowers and their bright colour scheme so vividly recall the flowers and plants of Augustan art (x, 550, 567) that one may well suppose them to be the copy of a much earlier work—unless indeed the mosaic was transferred from some earlier building that preceded the villa of the Antonine period. Not a few mosaics from the Villa of Hadrian, hitherto confidently dated to the Hadrianic period, seem much earlier in style. On this point see Hinks, *op. cit.* The technique of the present piece is astonishingly perfect, and the flowers are spread out in their yellow basket with consummate mastery.

[B. Nogara, *Mosaici Antichi del Laterano e dell Vaticano*, pl. XXXVII, 2; Helbig-Amelung, no. 315; E. Pfuhl, *Malerei u. Zeichnung der Griechen*, II, p. 863, fig. 704, who remarks on the rarity of flower pieces in ancient art; *id. Meisterwerke griechischer Zeichnung*, p. 87, fig. 151; E. Rizzo, pl. CLVII; R. Hinks, *B. M. Cat. Greek, etc. Paintings and Mosaics*, p. xvii. *Photograph Anderson*]

[*b*] MARBLE INTARSIA (*opus sectile*) with the Roman Lupercal, in *Rome, Palazzo Colonna*; found in 1838 in the territory of *Marino*. The panel of rosso antico is well preserved; the left upper corner was broken and put together already in Roman times. The once inserted coloured marble pieces have fallen out; the white body of the wolf, the yellow body of the child on the right and the white hook of the *pendum* are all that is preserved. In the picture are the *ficus ruminalis* with two birds (*picus* and *parra*); the shepherd *Faustulus*, gazing at the wolf and twins. The group may be that of the Palatine Lupercal, as restored by Augustus in honour of the legendary founders of Rome (x, 569). Above it an altar, presumably the one in front of the Lupercal, over which a bird flies from right to left in allusion to the happy auspices of Rome's foundation. On the left side is a high rock, above which sits Roma on her pile of armour and resting on her spear. The panel has been dated to the end of the second century B.C., but the emphatically Augustan symbolism—and the probability that the scene reproduces that of the Palatine Lupercal suggest a later Augustan or post-Augustan date. *Opus sectile* technique is on the whole uncommon; Pliny tells us that it came from the East in Hellenistic times and that it was used in Rome under Caesar, but that it became fashionable in the Claudian period and soon afterwards disappeared (*N.H.* XXXIV, 157; XXXVI, 47). We see it reappear three hundred years later in the *opus sectile* from the basilica of Junius Bassus in the Palazzo dei Conservatori. The panel, though published by Tomassetti, has been oddly overlooked as evidence for the Palatine Lupercal; nor has its importance for the reconstruction of the Lupercal panel of the Ara Pacis been taken into account.

[G. Tomasetti, *Röm. Mitt.* I, 1886, pp. 3 *sqq.*; and *Campagna Romana* (Via Latina), p. 183; E. Strong, *J.R.S.* I, 1911, pp. 3, 4; *Art in A.R.* II, fig. 297. *After a coloured drawing kindly lent by Prof. Francesco Tomassetti*]

[a]

[b]

HYPOGEUM AND COLUMBARIUM

[*a*] View of the interior of HYPOGEUM of Porta Maggiore on the Via Praenestina, *Rome*. The illustration looks towards the apse, and shows the nave with the pillars and the arches that separate it from the side aisles. This underground hall is situated at a depth of 40 ft. under the railway line, among monuments of the close of the first century and of the first half of the second; it is generally held to have been built and destroyed in the time of Claudius (A.D. 41–54), a date which accords with the building material and the style of decoration. The whole superficies of walls and pillars is covered with reliefs delicately executed in white stucco, representing mythological and ceremonial scenes, liturgical furniture and vessels, the whole apparently related to the discipline of the Soul in this world, in view of its ultramundane destiny. It was probably a hall of mystic initiation, possibly belonging to a villa with which it communicated by the long inclined passage way; or it may have been the seat of some religious or funerary *sodalitas*, connected with the adjacent burial grounds. Its reliefs are held to reflect Orphic or more especially Pythagorean doctrines. (x, 568, 582.)

[E. Strong and E. Joliffe in *J.H.S.* XLIV, 1924, pp. 65 *sqq.*; L. Wadsworth, Mem. Amer. *Acad*, IV, 1924, p. 79 *sq.*; J. Carcopino, *La Basilique Pythagoricienne de la Porte Majeure*, 1927; S. Bendinelli, *Monumenti dei Lincei*, 31, 1926, pp. 601 *sqq. Photograph American Academy*]

[*b*] Decorated apse of the COLUMBARIUM of Pomponius Hylas; found in Via Latina, *Rome*. The architectural features of the lower half are of interest. In the centre a small *aedicula* with niche for urns rises on a high podium containing a second niche for urns. On either side of the central *aedicula* are further niches with triangular pediments, broken in baroque style to hold a semicircular pediment in the centre. Among the subjects, which recall those of the Porta Maggiore Hypogeum, we find the following: on the wall above the niche of the central *aedicula*, the *cista mystica* flanked on either side by a man and a woman holding the roll of life (?); in the frieze is depicted Orpheus as *longa cum veste sacerdos*, among the Thracians; in the pediment a figure symbolizing the soul appears flanked by Tritons (*i.e.* Soul's voyage to the Isles of the Blest). The semidome or shell of the apse is decorated in colour on a white ground with tendrils and with three floating figures (the Soul between two Victories, emblems of her final triumph). The vine scrolls and tendrils, though painted in a rough rapid style, belong to the same repertory of vegetable and floral forms as those that decorate the deep bowls from Hildesheim. The whole hypogeum is covered with similar scenes. From one of the inscriptions (*C.I.L.* VI, 5540) and from the building material—concrete with brick facing—the columbarium is assigned to the period of Tiberius. (x, 567.)

[F. S. Newton, *P.B.S.R.* V, 1910, pp. 461 *sqq.* (with plates) with text by T. Ashby and a new mythological interpretation, including the Orpheus episode, by E. S[trong]; Wadsworth, *op. cit.* p. 38. *Photograph lent by German Institute*]

[a]

[b]

Stucco of semi-dome of the apse of the HYPOGEUM of Porta Maggiore. The stucco, which is much mutilated, is usually held to represent 'Sappho's Leap,' here symbolical of the liberation of the soul from the body. On the right Sappho, heavily draped and veiled and gently pushed by two Erotes, descends the fatal rock into a drapery held out in boat shape by a Triton or maybe a Siren, while on a high rock, in the middle distance, stands Apollo, holding out his right arm in a gesture of welcome. Recently Méautis has interpreted the Triton-Siren as Ino Leucothea. (x, 500, 568.)

[Literature as for 180, and Méautis in *Rev. Ét. Anciennes*, 1930, pp. 333 *sqq. After Monumenti dei Lincei*, 31, 1926, pl. XI]

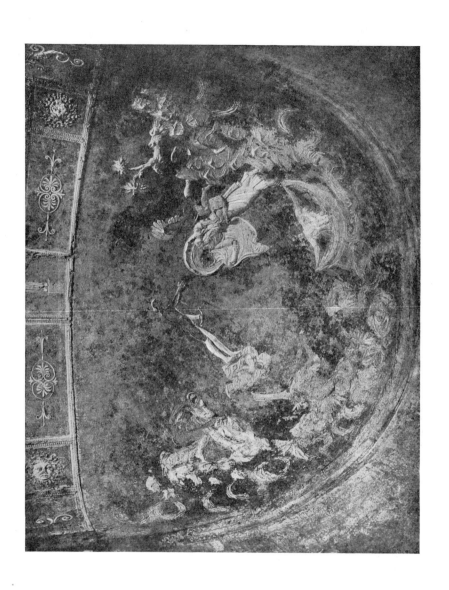

[*a*] SILVER PATERA with the glorification of agriculture; found at *Aquileia*; in *Vienna*. In the centre stands a prince (Claudius?) as Triptolemus, offering incense at the altar of Ceres, which is decorated with the Rape of Proserpine; his snake-driven chariot is waiting for him on his left and Ceres herself appears above on the right, seated under a tree. In the exergue reclines Terra Mater with a cow at her feet. At the top the figure of Caelus emerges from the clouds (cf. the cuirass of the Prima Porta statue, 150). The four seasons are in attendance: two seated on a ledge above on the left; two more on the right tending the snakes attached to the car of Triptolemus; the three children—two boys and a girl—who stand by the altar, the two boys holding up incense trays to the Emperor and the little girl carrying a basket of flowers on her head, are evidently conceived here as altar ministrants (*camilli*). The allegory is of the Earth's fertility under the Imperial rule (*fecunditas*), and as a result of the Emperor's care for agriculture. The basket of flowers on the ground on the left is treated with the same delicacy as the best Augustan flower pieces. Certain elements of the composition are inspired by, or even imitated from, Hellenistic compositions such as that of the celebrated Tazza Farnese (A. Furt-wängler, *Antike Gemmen*, Pls. 54, 55), but the whole has been re-moulded in the Roman crucible, and the composition centralized in the same manner as that of the cuirass of the Prima Porta statue or of the Grand Camée (156 [*b*]). Rostovtzeff well says: 'the *patera* admirably illustrates the way in which the emperors of the first century adhered to the ideas of Augustus and laid stress on being, like him, divine bringers of peace and prosperity, the great protectors and restorers of agriculture' (*Economic History of the Roman Empire*, text to pl. XII). (x, 569.)

[E. Loewy, 'Ein Römisches Kunstwerk' in *Festschrift für Strzygowski*, 1923, pp. 182 *sqq.*; cf. J. Toynbee, *The Hadrianic School*, p. 141]

[*b*] GLASS PASTE, with portrait of a Julio-Claudian prince and his three children; found at *Haidin*, near Pettau; in *Vienna*. The cameo is in two layers of blue, an upper and darker one on the lighter ground. The group is probably Nero Drusus with his three children: two boys, and the girl on the left (Germanicus, Claudius and Livilla?). For the central figure cf. the Nero Drusus (facing) of the cameo in British Museum (Bernoulli, *op. cit.* II, 1, pl. XXVI, II). The children shown as heads peeping from behind the principal figure, or as if cut off in front by the line of the medallion, produce a decorative effect. In the similar cameo in the British Museum (no. 1589), said to be of Germanicus with three of his sons, Nero, Drusus and Caligula, the little heads seem treated as phalerae. Several glass pastes of the same class have been found in Roman camps. (x, 570.)

[Eichler-Kris, no. 16, pl. 7 (with full bibliography). *Photographs Vienna Museum*]

[a]

[b]

FORA

[a] FORUM of AUGUSTUS and Temple of Mars in *Rome*. The illustration shows the southern side of the Forum with its hemicycle and part of the great area that surrounded the temple of Mars (see x, 578). The temple, its high Italic podium and four of its Corinthian columns of the right or south side are seen; the high flight of steps with the place for the altar is restored. On the right traces of the bases of the colonnaded portico. The square tower on the left of the illustration with loggia is a later medieval structure of the Knights of St John of Jerusalem.

[G. Lugli, *La zona archeologica*, 1931, p. 45; C. Ricci, *Capitolium*, VI, 1930, p. 157; *La Via dell' Impero*, p. 104]

[b] FORUM of CAESAR in *Rome*. The illustration shows the line of shops of tufa and travertine, which is all that remains of the time of Caesar. In front of the shops a colonnaded portico (the columns are now being re-erected), the remains of which, however, belong to the period of Honorius (A.D. 384–413). This portico possibly repeated one of the time of Trajan, which again may have followed the lines of an older portico of the time of Caesar. The temple, which was earlier in date than the forum, had been vowed by Caesar to Venus Genetrix at Pharsalus in 48 B.C. It lay on the central axis of the Forum but close to its lower end. An inscription found at Ostia (see x, 577) shows that what we now have of the temple belongs to the marble restoration of Trajan.

For a plan of the Forum see Plan 4 in Vol. x, facing p. 582; for the latest views as to the plan of the temple, which in the Trajanic period at any rate seems to have had an apse like that of Mars Ultor, see Brendel, *op. cit.*

[G. Lugli, *op. cit.* p. 43; C. Ricci, *Capitolium*, VIII, 1932, p. 157; *La Via dell' Impero*, p. 37; G. Calza, *Notizie degli Scavi*, 1932, p. 188 (for the inscription of Ostia); O. Brendel, *Archäol. Anz.* 1933, p. 617. *Photographs Governatorato*]

[a]

[b]

MONUMENTS

[*a*] TROPAEUM AUGUSTI (or Tropaeum Alpium), in the Alpes Maritimes, near the little town of *La Turbie*, which takes its name from the Tropaeum. (x, 572.) Tower-like monument supported on a quadrangular base (38 × 40 m. square and about 7 m. high); above this rises again a circular structure surrounded by columns, two of which are shown in our illustration replaced in their original position. (This was in 1909; since then the monument has been more completely restored.) Above this circular story rose, it is thought, a conical mound or else a stepped conical roof crowned either by a statue of Augustus or by a tropaeum. On the front of the base between figured reliefs was inserted the huge inscription (18 × 3 m.), recording that the monument was put up in honour of Augustus in 5 B.C. to commemorate the submission of forty-four Alpine peoples (*gentes alpinae devictae*) from the region between the Adriatic and the Mediterranean. The inscription has been put together out of very many fragments, with the help of the text preserved by Pliny (*N.H.* III, 34, 20). The monument was doubtless decorated by Imperial portraits. For portraits of Nero Drusus (d. 9 B.C.) and of his nephew Drusus Minor, son of Tiberius, probably set up at La Turbie, see F. Poulsen, *Sculptures Antiques de Musée de Province Espagnols*, 1933, pp. 43 *sqq.*

[*C.I.L.* v², no. 7817; Ph. Casimir, *Le trophée d'Auguste à La Turbie*, 1932, with numerous illustrations and a restoration by Formige]

[*b*] Part of the façade of the cavea of the THEATRE of MARCELLUS in *Rome* (as now restored). The building, which is of travertine and *opus reticulatum* in the foundations and inner parts, was covered with stucco and marble. In its three arcaded stories it shows—like the Colosseum (cf. the Tabularium)—the alternation of Doric, Ionic and Corinthian in the half-columns between the arcades. The theatre is said to have held about 14,000 spectators. (For a further description see x, 574.)

[G. Lugli, *op. cit.* p. 341; Platner-Ashby, p. 513; M. Bieber, *Denkmäler zum Theaterwesen*, 1920, p. 59 *sq.*, pl. 26, plan fig. 61]

[a]

[b]

[a], [b] RELIEFS with façades of first-century TEMPLES; *Villa Medici, Rome.* [a] Restored: part of the podium and of the pediment; various parts of the columns. Probably the temple of the *Magna Mater* on the Palatine rebuilt by Augustus in A.D. 3 (cf. Platner-Ashby, p. 324). In the pediment the altar of the *Magna Mater* covered with a veil; at either side a priest, the *Gallus*; in the angles are panthers *couchant*. The corner-acroteria formed by two dancing corybants. (x, 575.) This is part of the frieze discussed and illustrated above, 126. [b] Restored: most of the steps; the first column on the left with the corner of the pediment and the Victory; half of the first and second column on the right and parts of the others. Probably the octastyle temple of Mars Ultor in the Forum of Augustus on a high flight of steps. In the pediment stands a bearded figure with high-crested helmet, sceptre, and sword, thought to be the *Divus Romulus*, with Venus and Fortuna on either side and surrounded by four seated figures in the angles of the pediment (local divinities?). The corner-acroteria are Victories. (x, 578.)

[E. Petersen, *Ara Pacis*, pl. III, 13, 7; E. Strong, *loc. cit.* p. 69. *Photographs German Institute*]

[c] Fragment of RELIEF with temple-façade, in the *Museo Mussolini, Rome.* Façade set obliquely to the spectator; Ionic columns on a high flight of steps. From the place where it was found this is conjecturally attributed to the *Arcus* erected to Claudius across the *Via Lata* in A.D. 51/52 after the subjection of Britain. The advanced style may well be Julio-Claudian. Found in 1925 together with other fragments under the Corso, near the church of San Marcello.

[G. Mancini, *Notizie degli Scavi*, 1925, p. 234; E. Strong, *Art in Ancient Rome*, I, p. 164; for the arch of Claudius, cf. Platner-Ashby, p. 35. *Photograph from Prof. Bocconi*]

[d] Sepulchral MONUMENT, from *Chieti* (reconstruction), in *Rome, Museo delle Terme.* The reliefs, the inscription and some fragments of the architecture—which probably formed a little *templum in antis*—are all that is preserved. The inscription records this as the tomb of a *sevir augustalis C. Lusius Storax,* who had erected it for himself, his three wives and the joint owners of the tomb (*socii monumenti*). The reliefs refer to an episode in the life of Storax, who as *sevir* would have to offer public spectacles. Here he presides at a gladiatorial fight, seated in the middle of the pediment surrounded by dignitaries, musicians, and spectators and attended by two lictors. The gladiatorial contest is unfolded along the frieze of the architrave. The monument is probably Claudian. The style is provincial and the manner of filling the pediment with a frontal composition is non-classical. Traces of columns show that a building filled the upper part of the pediment as a background. Not discussed in text, but illustrated for contrast between Italic, provincial style and the classical manner of the temples, 190 [a, b, c].

[Helbig-Amelung, no. 1526, with older bibliography; E. Strong, *op. cit.* p. 172; Paribeni, pl. CLVII (the portrait). *Photograph supplied by Prof. Giglioli*]

[a]

[b]

[c]

[d]

[a] ARCH of RIMINI (*Ariminum*), 27 B.C. According to the inscription erected to commemorate the reconstruction by Augustus
of the most important roads of Italy. It is placed where the Via
Flaminia enters Rimini and served as a monumental entrance in
front of the city gate. The archivolt rests on plain pilasters; framed
at either side by half-corinthian columns, set against pillars; above
the keystone is carved a bull's head, as on many Etruscan gates.
The plain frieze supports a small pediment awkwardly placed without resting on the columns. The attica bears the long inscription.
In the spandrels medallions with heads of Neptune and Mars on
the south side; Juppiter and Apollo or Venus (?) on the north. The
arch carried a statue of Augustus like the arch on the Ponte Milvio
of Rome (Cassius Dio LIII, 22). The crenellations are medieval.

[*C.I.L.* XI, 365; I. A. Richmond, 'Commemorative arches and city gates in the
Augustan Age' in *J.R.S.* XXIII, 1933, pp. 159 *sqq.*; F. Noack, 'Vorträge Bibliothek
Warburg', 1925–6, pp. 170, 175, pl. 1, 2; T. Ashby-R. Fell, 'The Via Flaminia' in
J.R.S. XI, 1921, p. 189. For restoration of the Flaminian Way see X, 119; *Res
Gestae*, 20]

[b] ARCH of SUSA (*Segusio*), 8 B.C., facing city. Put up in the
Cottian Alps in honour of the recognition of the prince Cottius as
ruler for Rome of that region (X, 215). At the corners Corinthian
columns. On the frieze ceremonies connected with the ratification.
The attica, once bearing the inscription, probably supported statues.

[*C.I.L.* V, 7231; Ferrero, *L'arc d'Auguste à Suse*; F. Studniczka, *Arch. Jahrb.*
1903, pp. 1 *sqq.*; E. Loewy, 'Die Anfänge des Triumphbogens', in *Jahrb. Kunsthist.
Samml. in Wien*, N.F. Sonderheft II, 1928, pp. 9 *sqq.*; F. Noack, *op. cit.* p. 173]

[c] ARCH of FANO (*Fanum Fortunae*), A.D. 9/10, facing country,
spanning the Via Flaminia, dedicated to Agustus who had walled
the city. The arch was a façade to the city gate. Once it had three
passage ways and was flanked by two round-fronted towers, one
of which on the right has disappeared under the church of S.
Michele, built in 1495. A drawing of its original shape is preserved
on the wall of the church. The superstructure rose in several
stories, cf. the Augustan arch of Turin (*Porta Palatina*). Restored
in the time of Constantine.

[*C.I.L.* XI, 6218, 6219; Richmond, *op. cit.* pp. 156 *sqq.*; Ashby-Fell, *op. cit.* p. 188.
Photographs Alinari]

[d] ARCH of ORANGE (*Arausio*) of A.D. 25 (?), north side; probably
associated with a triple city-gate which it screened. Date and style
of reliefs have given rise to discussion. Perhaps late Caesarian or
early Augustan; the inscription of the architrave in honour of
Tiberius and his victory over Sacrovir, datable to A.D. 21, belongs
to a later restoration. On the frieze of the architrave is a battle
between Gauls and Romans. On the *fasciae* of the architrave are
plug-holes for the bronze lettering of the inscription. (X, 579.)

[*C.I.L.* XII, 1230; P. Couissin, *Rev. Arch.* XXIV, 1926, pp. 210 *sqq.*; E. Espérandieu,
Recueil gén. des Bas Reliefs de la Gaule Romaine; F. Noack, *op. cit.* pp. 176 *sqq.*,
pls. 6–7, 11–12; E. Loewy, *op. cit.* pp. 13 *sqq.*; Richmond, *op. cit.* p. 152]

[a]

[b]

[c]

[d]

COINS OF OCTAVIAN, ANTONY
AND CLEOPATRA

[a] *Octavian*, aureus, 41 B.C. C · CAESAR · COS · PONT · AVG. His head bare. Rev. Head of Julius Caesar, laureate, the Julian star over his forehead. Wt. 8·06 g. (x, 17, 578.)

[b] *Lucius Antonius*, denarius, 41 B.C. Head of his brother Antony with augural lituus. Rev. PIETAS COS, figure of Pietas. Wt. 3·9 g. (x, 28.)

[c] *Antony and Octavian*, denarius, 41 B.C. Their heads on either side; a *capis* behind that of Antony, an augural lituus behind that of Octavian. Wt. 8·06 g. (x, 17, 32.)

[d]–[f] Portraits of *Cleopatra*. [d] A silver drachma minted in Alexandria in 47 B.C. The queen at the age of twenty-three. Wt. 2·97 g. [e] Bronze coin, issued some years later. Both coins with Ptolemaic eagle on reverse. (x, 35.) [f] Bronze. Bust of Aphrodite diademed holding Eros, a sceptre at her shoulder (Cleopatra and Ptolemy Caesar). Rev. Double cornucopiae. (x, 37.) *B.M.C. Ptolemies*, p. 122 sq., 1, 9, 2.

[g]–[i] Bronze coins issued by Antony's fleet-prefects in 36 to 35 B.C. [g], [h] Heads of Antony and Octavia. [i] Similar with Octavian's head conjoined to Antony's, Octavia facing them. Revs. [g] Poseidon and Amphitrite in a quadriga of hippocamps. [h], [i] War-galleys under sail. (x, 52, 59.)

[j] *Sextus Pompeius*, denarius minted in Sicily, *c.* 38 B.C. NEPTVNI, head of Pompey the Great as Neptune with trident and dolphin. Rev. War-galley under sail. Wt. 4·0 g. (x, 57.)

[k], [l] *Antony*, denarii. [k] *c.* 42 B.C. after Philippi. Head of Antony, unshaven in token of mourning for Julius. Rev. Head of Helios radiate. [l] 37 B.C. Antony as augur. Rev. The same as last, the type deliberately revived. Wt. 3·85, 3·78 g. (x, 68.)

All in the *British Museum*.

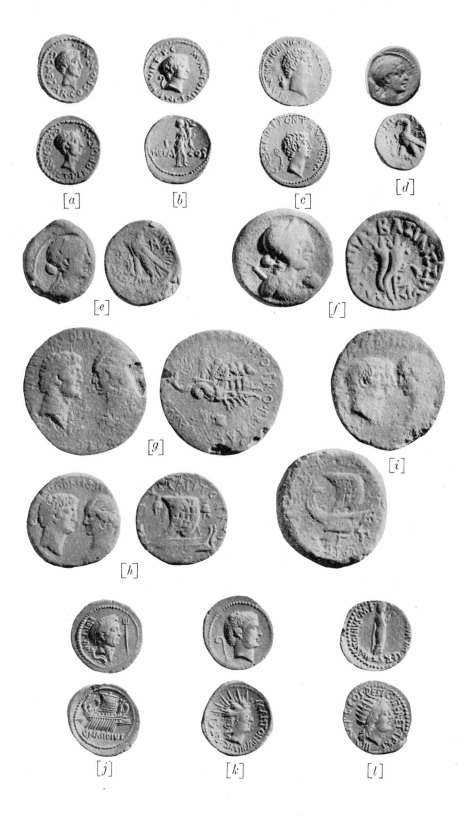

[a] [b] [c] [d]

[e] [f]

[g] [i]

[h]

[j] [k] [l]

[a]–[h] Issues of *Antony*. [a] Denarius, c. 40 B.C. Rev. caduceus on globe between two opposed cornuacopiae (see 124 [b] above), perhaps a reference to the union of Antony and Octavia. [b] Cistophoric tetradrachm minted in the Province of Asia, c. 39 B.C. His head within ivy-wreath. Rev. Bust of Octavia over *cista* between serpents (cf. Volume of Plates iii, 14 [f], [h]). (x, 69.) [c] Denarius, 36 B.C. Rev. Armenian tiara and bow. (x. 72.) [d], [e] Denarii representing two of the thirty series of legionary coins, c. 32 to 31 B.C. Legionary eagle between two standards. Rev. Antony's flagship; [d] LEG XVI, [e] LEG · XVII · CLASSICAE. (x, 78, 100.) [f] Denarius minted probably in Alexandria, 34 B.C., commemorating the Donations of Alexandria. Antony's head, Armenian tiara behind it; legend 'Armenia conquered.' Rev. Bust of Cleopatra as 'Queen of kings and of her sons who are kings.' (x, 80, 81.) [g] Aureus, c. 35/34 B.C., with heads of Antony and his elder son by Fulvia, M. Antonius the younger, nicknamed Antyllus. (x, 81.) [h] Denarius minted by Decimus Turillius in 31 B.C. after Antony had been hailed *Imperator* for the fourth time. Rev. A Victory. (x, 101.) Wts. 3·76, 12·25, 3·88, 3·4, 3·53, 3·58, 8·0, 3·8 g.

[i], [j] *Octavian's triumph*, denarii struck, after Actium, in the East, 31 to 29 B.C. [i] Bust of Victory. Rev. Neptune, foot on globe. [j] Octavian in triumphal quadriga. Rev. Victory on prow (cf. Volume of Plates ii, 10 [k]). Wts. 3·67, 3·98 g. (x, 113.)

[k], [l] *Agrippa* in Gaul, c. 39/38 B.C. The earliest certain evidence for the use by Octavian of the praenomen of *Imperator*. [k] Aureus with head of Julius; [l] denarius with heads of Julius and Octavian. On both reverses, M · AGRIPPA · COS/DESIG. Wts. 8·2, 3·92g. (x, 122.)

[m], [n] Silver coins of the *Himyarites* of South Arabia modelled on Athenian money. [m] Third to second century B.C. Head of Athene Rev. Owl. [n] c. 100 to 24 B.C. Laureate male head in wreath. Rev. Owl. Wts. 5·39, 5·50 g. (x, 249.)

[o] *Augustus*, aureus, 18 B.C. Head of Liber. Rev. AVGVSTO/OB · c(ives) · s(ervatos) with a *corona civica*. Wt. 8·05 g. (x, 130.)

All in the *British Museum*.

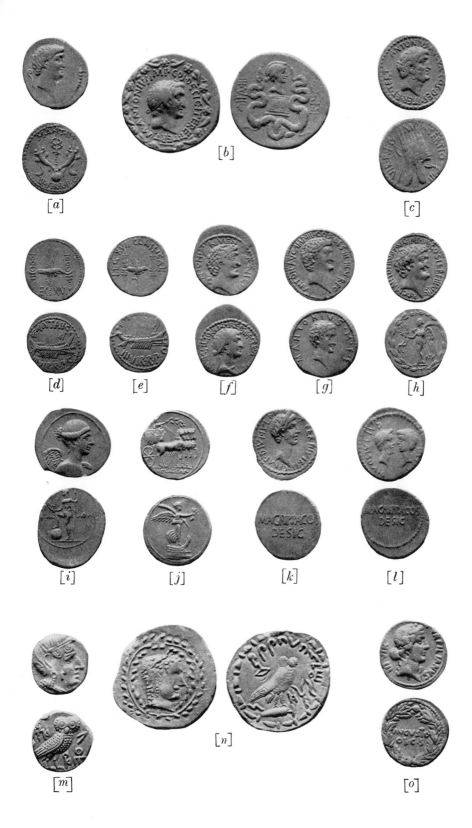

[a]

[b]

[c]

[d]

[e]

[f]

[g]

[h]

[i]

[j]

[k]

[l]

[m]

[n]

[o]

[a]–[c] Coins of *Augustus*. [a] Denarius, 18 B.C. Bust of Feronia. Rev. Parthian kneeling in the act of surrendering a standard. [b] Aureus, 18/17 B.C. Head of Augustus. Rev. CIVIB · ET · SIGN · MILIT · A · PART · RECVP. Triumphal arch. (x, 263.) [c] Denarius, 18 B.C. Bust of Virtus. Rev. Armenian kneeling in submission. (x, 264.) Wts. 3·81, 7·82, 4·04 g. [b] a Spanish mint, [a], [c] Rome.

[d] *Phraataces*, king of *Parthia* (3 B.C. to A.D. 4), and his mother, *Thea Urania Musa*, an Italian slave-girl who had become the legitimate queen of Phraates (38 to 3 B.C.). Drachma. Head of Phraataces between two Victories. Rev. Bust of Queen Musa. Wt. 3·65 g. (x, 265.)

[e]–[n] Roman coins with types of religious interest. [e] Denarius of the moneyer L. Valerius Acisculus, *c.* 45 B.C. Head of Apollo Soranus, a little hammer (*acisculus*) behind. Rev. Head of Aphrodisian Sibyl. [f] Silver sestertius minted by C. Considius Paetus in *c.* 45 B.C. Winged bust of Cupid. Rev. Two cornuacopiae on globe (cf. 198 [a]). [g] Aureus struck by P. Clodius M.f., *c.* 43, or 38 B.C. Head of Helios (cf. 196 [k], [l]). Rev. Crescent and planets. (x, 472.) Wts. 3·98, 0·76, 8·1 g. [h] Aureus of 43/42, or 39 B.C. Head of Octavian. Rev. Aeneas carrying Anchises. [i] Aureus of *c.* 43 or 38 B.C. Head as last. Rev. Venus seated on cippus, Cupid beside her. (x, 473.) Wts. 8·1, 8·09 g. [j] Aureus, 17 B.C. A Herald. Rev. Head of the youthful deified Julius, the *Sidus Julium* above. [k] Aureus, 16 B.C. Head of Augustus. Rev. Augustus on a platform distributing to the people the means of purification. [l] Denarius, 16 B.C. Head as last. Rev. Apollo on a platform ornamented with prows and anchors. [m] Denarius, 16 B.C. Head as last. Rev. Cippus with inscription. [n] Denarius, 16 B.C. In wreath I · O · M · /S · P · Q · R · V · S · /PR · S · IMP · CAE · /QVOD · PER · EV · /R · PIN AMP · /AT · Q · TRAN · /S · E. Rev. Cippus, IMP/CAES/ AVGV/COMM/CONS/. Wts. 7·89, 8·01, 3·93, 3·47, 3·56 g. (x, 478.)

[o] *Augustus*, aureus of 12 B.C. when he became Pontifex Maximus. His head. Rev. The gate of his house, with oak-wreath above, laurels at each side. Wt. 8·00 g. (x, 479.) [p] Quinarius, 29/27 B.C. His head. Rev. ASIA RECEPTA, Victory on *cista* between serpents (cf. 198 [b]). Wt. 1·91 g. (x, 114.)

[q] *Gaius*, dupondius of A.D. 40/41. Nero and Drusus Caesar as Dioscuri on horseback. Rev. Inscription round s · c. This illustrates the tendency to compare Imperial princes with the Dioscuri. (Cf. Gaius and Lucius, *B.M.C. Rom. Emp.* i, pp. 88, 513 *sqq.*; sons of Drusus, 202 [g]). (x, 624.)

All in the *British Museum*.

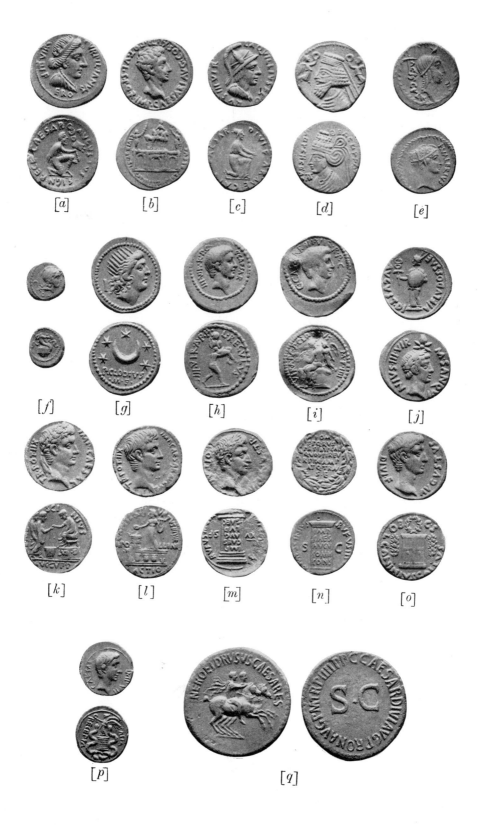

[a]   [b]   [c]   [d]   [e]

[f]   [g]   [h]   [i]   [j]

[k]   [l]   [m]   [n]   [o]

[p]   [q]

[a], [b] *Juba II*, king of Mauretania, 25 B.C.–A.D. 23. Denarii with his portrait. Revs. [a] Temple of Augustus, [b] Altar between trees, LVCVS AVGVSTI. Wts. 2·92, 3·23 g. (x, 488.)

[c], [d] The deification of Augustus under *Tiberius*. [c] Aureus. Head of Tiberius. Rev. Head of Augustus, a star above. Wt. 7·79 g. [d] As. Head of Augustus radiate. Rev. Eagle on glove. (x, 611.)

[e] *Nero* with a radiate crown. Dupondius of A.D. 64–66. Rev. Victory. (x, 501.)

All in the *British Museum*.

[f] Sestertius minted at *Romula* in Spain with heads of Tiberius and Livia. She appears as IULIA AVGVSTA GENETRIX ORBIS. In the *Bibliothèque Nationale*.

[g], [h] Sestertii of *Tiberius*. [g] A.D. 22/23. Caduceus between opposed cornuacopiae, from each of which projects the bust of a child, twin sons of Drusus and Livilla. Rev. s · c. and legend (x, 624.) [h] A.D. 22/23. CIVITATIBVS ASIAE RESTITVTIS. Tiberius on Curule chair. Rev. as last. (x, 651.)

[i] *Smyrna*, bronze, A.D. 29 to 35. Busts of the Senate and Livia face to face. Rev. Temple containing the statue of Tiberius. (x, 651.)

[j] *Ptolemaïs-Ace* as a Colony. Bronze. Head of Nero. Rev. The Emperor Claudius ploughing as founder; behind the team the standards of four legions (III, VI, X, XII), the last only legible. (x, 679.)

[g] to [j] in the *British Museum*.

[*a*]–[*c*] *Nero*, Imperial coinage, A.D. 64 to 68. [*a*] Sestertius. Rev. Roma. [*b*] Aureus. Rev. Temple of Vesta. Wt. 7·29 g. [*c*] Dupondius. Rev. Front view of a large building, the Macellum. (x, 733.)

[*d*]–[*h*] *Alexandria*, tetradrachms of Nero all of his fourteenth regnal year (A.D. 67/68). Radiate bust of the Emperor wearing the aegis of Zeus. On the reverses. [*d*] 'Zeus Olympios,' [*e*] 'Zeus Nemeios,' [*f*] 'Hera Argeia,' [*g*] 'Poseidon Isthmios,' [*h*] 'Apollon Pytheios.' (x, 737.)

[*i*]–[*m*] *British* gold coins. [*i*] *Verica*, son of Commius. Vine-leaf. Rev. Horseman. [*j*] *Cunobelinus*. CAMV, Ear of corn. Rev. CVNO, horse. Wts. 5·31, 5·35 g. (x, 793.) [*k*], [*l*] *Dubnovellaunus*. Stylized pattern. Rev. Horse over a branch. [*m*] *Tincommius*, similar but cruder, wheel under horse. Wts. 5·25, 5·38, 5·36 g. (x, 794.)

[*n*] *Galba*, aureus, A.D. 68/69. Mint of Rome. His head. Rev. SALVS GEN HVMANI, female figure, foot on globe, sacrificing at altar. Wt. 7·03 g. (x, 811.)

[*o*]–[*q*] *Vitellius*, A.D. 69. [*o*] Denarius of Rome. His head. Rev. Bust of his father, Lucius Vitellius. [*p*], [*q*] Aurei of Lugdunum. Reverses: FIDES EXERCITVVM, clasped hands; and, CONSENSVS EXERCITVVM, Mars. Wts. 3·19, 5·91, 7·30 g. (x, 818, 827.)

All in the *British Museum*.

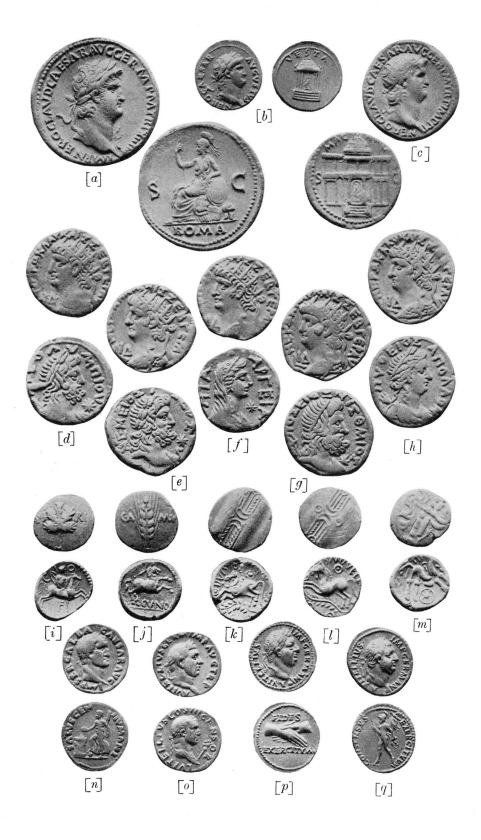

[a]

[b]

[c]

[d]

[e]

[f]

[g]

[h]

[i]

[j]

[k]

[l]

[m]

[n]

[o]

[p]

[q]

[a], [b] *L. Clodius Macer*, denarii minted in Africa, A.D. 68. [a] His head. Rev. War-galley. Wt. 5·06 g. [b] ROMA, head of Roma. Rev. Trophy. [a] *Brit. Mus.* [b] *Copenhagen Nat. Mus.* (x, 812.)

[c] *Germanicus* in the East. Didrachm minted in Caesarea in Cappadocia probably under Gaius in A.D. 37/38, but referring to A.D. 18. Head of Germanicus. Rev. Germanicus, nearly facing, placing a tiara on the head of King Artaxias, who stands facing. Wt. 7·67 g. (x, 621, 747.) In *Berlin*.

[d] *Antiochus IV* of Commagene, bronze, A.D. 38 to 72. His head. Rev. ΛΥΚΑΟΝΩΝ, Scorpion, all in wreath. (x, 750.)

[e] *Ajax*, high-priest of Olba and Governor of Lalassis and Cennatis, bronze, A.D. 10 to 14. His head as Hermes. Rev. Triskeles, *A* (=year 1). (x, 744.)

[f] *Polemo*, high priest of Olba, etc., bronze, between A.D. 17 and 36. His head. Rev. A throne, **IA** (=year 11). (x, 752.) [d] to [f] in the *British Museum*.

[g] He was still ruling under *Galba*, as is proved by a bronze coin with head of Galba. Rev. Athena standing facing. (x, 774.) *Bibliothèque Nationale*.

[h]–[n] Coins of the *Bosporan Kingdom*. [h] Queen *Gepaepyris*, bronze, c. A.D. 39. Her bust. Rev. Female bust wearing calathus. [i] *Gepaepyris* and her stepson *Mithridates* (*VIII*), c. A.D. 40. Bust on either side. (x, 751.) [j] Queen *Dynamis*, gold stater, 17/16 B.C. Her head. Rev. The star and crescent, emblem of the royal house of Pontus (cf. 2 [m], 4 [a]–[d]). Wt. 8·03 g. (x, 267.) [k] *Dynamis*, gold stater, 8 B.C. Head of Augustus. Rev. Head of Agrippa, date, and monogram of Dynamis. Wt. 7·99 g. (x, 269.) [l] *Mithridates* (*VIII*), gold stater, A.D. 39/40. Head of Gaius. Rev. Nike with wreath and palm. Wt. 7·85 g. (x, 751.) [m] Bosporan gold stater of A.D. 62/63. Head of Claudius. Rev. Head and monogram of Nero. There is no reference to King Cotys. Wt. 7·96 g. (x, 775.) [n] *Rhescuporis*, gold stater, A.D. 68/69. Head of Vespasian. Rev. Head of Titus and monogram. [l], *Jameson Coll.*; [n] formerly *Grand Duke Alexander Michailovich Coll.*; [m] *Hermitage*; [h], [i], [k], *British Museum*; [j], formerly *Countess Uvarov Coll.*

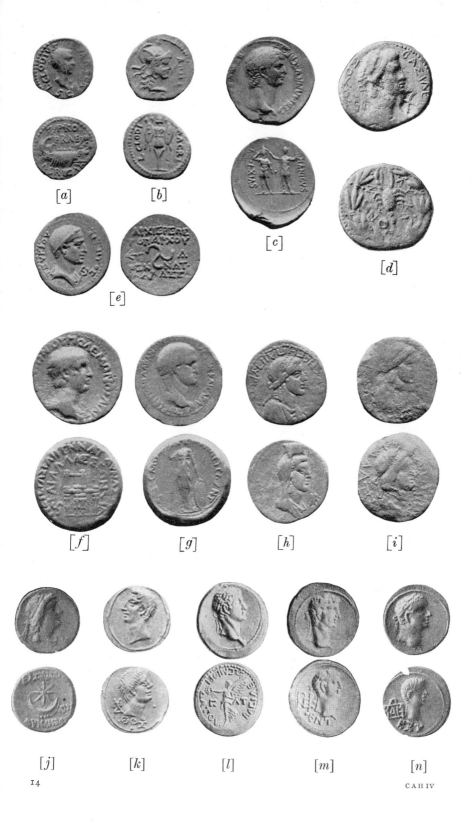

[a] [b] [c] [d]

[e]

[f] [g] [h] [i]

[j] [k] [l] [m] [n]

[a] *Augustus*, denarius, 19 to 15 B.C. His head. Rev. Temple and statue of Juppiter Tonans. (x, 575.) [b] *Cn. Domitius Ahenobarbus*, aureus, 42/41 B.C. His head. Rev. Temple of Neptune. (x, 573.) [c] *Augustus*, aureus, 36 B.C. His head. Rev. Temple and statue of the Divine Julius. (x, 576.) [d] *Augustus*, aureus, 18/17 B.C. His head. Rev. Circular temple and statue of Mars Ultor. (x, 575.) [e] *Claudius*, aureus, A.D. 41 to 45. Head of Nero Drusus. Rev. Triumphal arch inscribed DE GERM. (x, 579.) Wts. 3·80, 8·16, 8·06, 7·90, 7·69 g.

[f] *Augustus*, sestertius of Lugdunum, c. A.D. 10 to 14. His head. Rev. The altar of 'Roma et Augustus' at Lugdunum. (x, 198, 553.)

[g] *Octavian*, aureus, c. 39 B.C. His head. Rev. Equestrian statue. Wt. 7·93 g. (x, 563.) [h] *Claudius*, denarius, A.D. 46/47. His head. Rev. Arch as on [e] above. Wt. 3·64 g.

[i] *Tiberius*, sestertius, A.D. 36/37. Temple of Concord and her statue within; on the flanking walls, Hercules and Mercury; on the roof the Capitoline Triad between Diana and Ceres, flanked at each end by Victories. Rev. s · c, and legend. (x, 577, 580.) [j] *Nero*, bronze as, A.D. 64–66. His head. The 'Ara Pacis.' (x, 546.)

All in the *British Museum*.

[k] *Parthia*, tetradrachm of A.D. 54/55 assigned by some to a pretender. Bust of a king. Rev. Tyche standing before the enthroned king. (x, 879.) In the *Bibliothèque Nationale*.

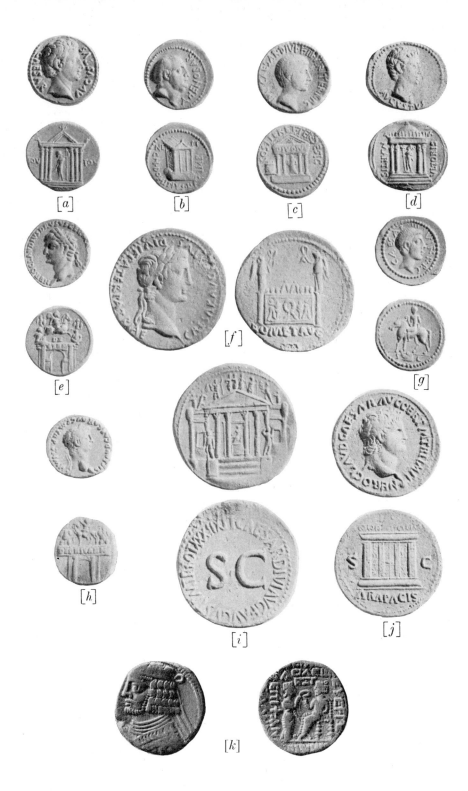

[a]　　　　[b]　　　　[c]　　　　[d]

[e]　　　　[f]　　　　[g]

[h]　　　　[i]　　　　[j]

[k]